THE ULTIMATE
CRAPPER
COMPANION

Explosive Trivia, Bathroom Games and
Other Cool Stuff To Keep You Entertained
While You Poop

Bill O'Neill

ISBN: 978-1-64845-133-1
Copyright © 2025 By LAK Publishing
ALL RIGHTS RESERVED

The illustrations in this book were designed
using images from Freepik.com.

CONTENTS

INTRODUCTION

Did you know there was once a man named Thomas Crapper?

And did you know that Mr. Crapper was one of Victorian England's most famous plumbers, sewage workers, and plumbing businessmen?

In fact, as well as making several improvements to the cistern and the workings of the flush toilet, Thomas Crapper ran a hugely successful plumbing and toilet factory in central London, from where his company sold everything from U-bends and ballcocks to drain covers and sewage pipes. If you were to wander around the streets of Westminster in the center of London today, moreover, you might still see a manhole in the middle of the sidewalk with Crapper's name stamped onto it!

The fact that Mr. Thomas Crapper genuinely existed—plus the fact that he spent his entire life improving our toilets and sewage networks—has led some people to believe his name is the reason why toilets today are known as "crappers." It's a nice theory, certainly. Unfortunately, it's not true.

The true story here is a lot less surprising (and a lot less pleasant). In fact, the word *crap* has been used since medieval times to refer to waste material of any kind, from the dregs left in the bottom of a beer barrel to the chaff left over after threshing corn. Our domestic toilet merely became known as the "crapper" because—well, let's just say it's where our "crap" ends up.

And, hey—that's where you are now, right? Taking some time in the crapper. Which is good news, too, because that is precisely where this book comes in handy!

This is *The Ultimate Crapper Companion*—a unique compendium of fascinating stories, random facts, puzzles, games, and mind-bending brainteasers. All the stories and games here all divided into nice, short, fun, easy-to-digest, one-page sections—just the right length to take in a page or two while you're on the toilet.

To put it another way, the point of this book is to make sure the time you spend in the crapper isn't wasted...

THE WORLD'S FIRST PRANK PHONE CALL

T hey're the go-to practical joke of pranksters the world over. Call up someone's number, and come up with some ludicrous story, some ridiculous fake name, or some silly one-liner before hanging up and laughing yourself silly.

For a long time, the staple prank phone call was, of course, to phone someone up and ask them if their refrigerator is running. (Setting yourself up for the killer punchline, "Well, you better get after it then!") But back in the day, telephone pranksters had other lines up their sleeves—which is just as well, to be honest, because astonishingly the very first prank phone call predates the first household electric refrigerator by more than two decades!

Incredibly, the first recorded prank phone calls date back to 1884 (when the telephone itself was barely eight years old!). According to regional news articles published at the time, almost 150 years ago pranksters would keep themselves entertained by (rather morbidly) calling up local undertakers and mortuaries, requesting their services for the collection of a dead body. The unknowing undertakers and their assistants would then understandably do precisely what was being asked of them and would turn up to the requested address armed with their blankets, candles, ice bags, a coffin, and all the other kit they would need to transport a corpse. It was only then that they would discover that the person they had come to collect was alive and well, and that they had been the butt of a rather annoying (and massively time-wasting) joke.

For the pranksters, to pull off a ruse like this was a rather daring escapade in the late 1800s, as telephones were still so uncommon, and still so rarely found in people's homes, that they would likely have to make the fake call for assistance from a public phone booth—the kind of thing that might then only have been found in a nearby train station, the entrance of a local restaurant, or by the reception desk of a hotel. The call would also have to be patched through a bank of human operators, who would quite literally connect the prankster's line to that of the undertaker, and in doing so would know precisely where the incoming call was coming from, allowing the prankster to be potentially easily tracked down.

Whether anyone ever was apprehended for their prank phone calls—and quite why undertakers seemed to so commonly be the butt of the joke, for that matter—is unfortunately not recorded in the same papers that first reported on these pranks way back in the 1880s. But after a few years, the fad had moved on, and telephone pranksters had turned their attention elsewhere.

As it became ever more common for businesses to be connected to the burgeoning telephone network, they began listing their telephone number on their business cards and other literature. Ultimately, pranksters began leaving fake calling cards and other notelets with different offices and individuals, saying that they had tried to see them but had presumably missed them. The hapless victim would then, following the instructions on their apparent visitor's card, unknowingly telephone the local station asking to speak to a "Mr. Train," or call up the local aquarium looking to speak to a "Mr. Fish."

Pranking, it seems, is nothing new!

TOP 6 · FACTS
PHONES AND PHONE CALLS

- A survey in 2022 found that there are now more mobile telephones in the world than there are people to use them!

- The world's first telephone call was made by Scottish inventor Alexander Graham Bell, who used a prototype device in his laboratory to phone up his assistant in another room, saying, "Mr Watson, come here, I want to see you."

- Although Bell is credited with inventing the telephone, you can thank Thomas Edison for how we answer it. The two inventors raced to corner the telecommunications market in the mid 1800s, and as both their businesses began to grow, Bell proposed that the word used to answer a ringing telephone should be the sailor's greeting, "Ahoy!" Edison, however, preferred "Hello!" and we've been answering the telephone that way ever since!

- As for the word *telephone* itself, it actually predates the telephone. The French inventor François Sudre coined the word *telephone* in the early 1800s as the name of a bizarre long-distance communication system that used coded musical notes to transmit messages.

- The world's first mobile telephone was invented in 1983. Its battery only lasted 30 minutes, however, and it took 10 hours to recharge it!

- In 2003, a US radio host pranked then-president of Venezuela, Hugo Chavez, by telephoning his office pretending to be then-president of Cuba, Fidel Castro. Once he had got through to the Venezuelan leader on air, the host then tried the opposite—and got through to Fidel Castro pretending to be Hugo Chavez!

How quickly can you solve this crossword?

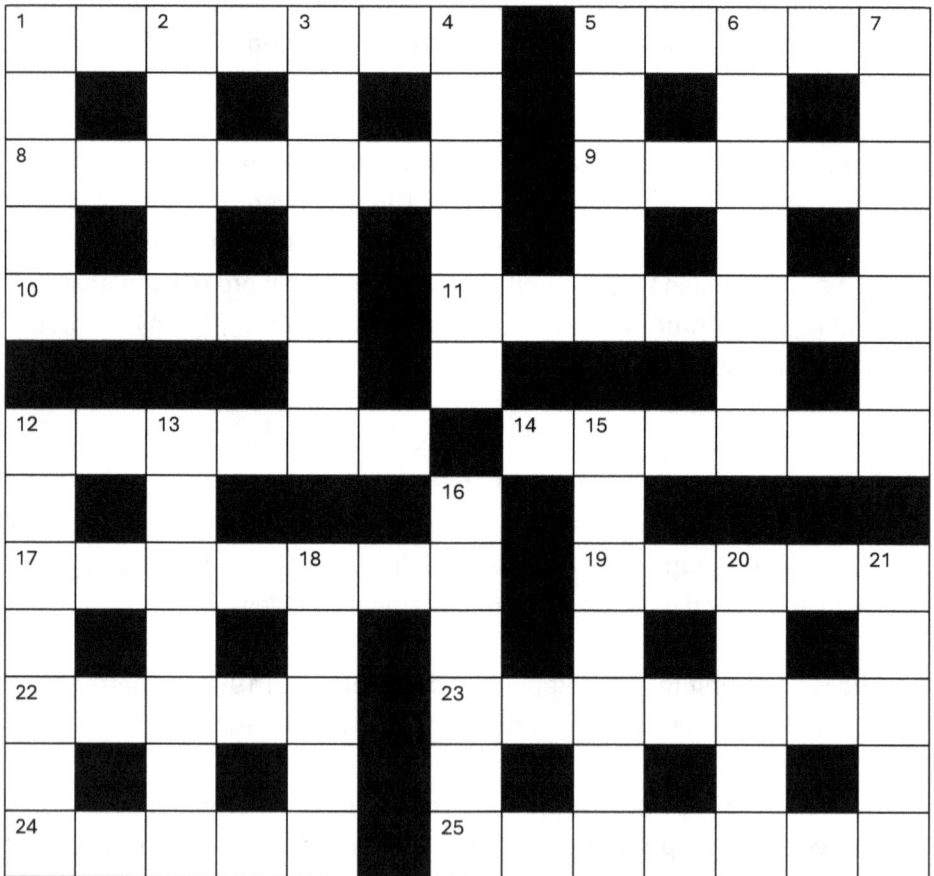

ACROSS

1. Ask
5. Atmospheres
8. Place for skating
9. Church table
10. Feel
11. Continuous
12. Imp
14. Fails to hit
17. Bison
19. Foolish
22. Painter's stand
23. Congestion on the roads
24. Errands
25. Where a movie is made, say

DOWN

1. Train tracks
2. King's wife
3. Obvious
4. Pinching, stealing
5. Once more
6. Turns
7. Screenplays
12. Topic
13. Says no
15. Add a program to a computer system, say
16. Kinda
18. Book of maps
20. Raises
21. Sailboat

Each of the 5-letter words below is missing its middle letter. Place those missing letters in the corresponding spaces in the grid, and a 7-letter word will be revealed reading down the central column. Watch out, though—there might be more than one possible missing letter for some words, but there is only one possible solution.

▼

W	H		L	E
N	A		E	S
S	T		T	E
U	R		E	D
P	R		N	T
M	O		T	H
T	H		I	R

What word is being implied by the image below?

MOTION

THE TROUBLED PRODUCTION OF THE WIZARD OF OZ

I t's one of the best-known, best-loved, and most-admired movies of all time. In fact, it is now so popular that the US Library of Congress estimates it to be the most-watched film in cinema history. Not only that, but it was nominated for five Oscars (winning one, for Best Song, for "Over the Rainbow"), while its 16-year-old star, Judy Garland, so impressed the glitterati of Hollywood at the time that she was awarded a special child-sized Academy Award for her performance. But despite its long string of accolades, and the generations of people it has entertained, at the time, *The Wizard of Oz* had one of the most notoriously difficult productions in movie history.

The problems all began at the casting stage, with Judy Garland reportedly vying against a handful of fellow child stars—including Hollywood veteran Shirley Temple—for the role of Dorothy. Contractual issues meant the role eventually went to Garland, despite Temple being the bigger box office draw—but Garland's contract, and her age, meant that she went into filming earning one of the lowest salaries out of all of the cast. According to some reports, while the dwarf actors playing the Munchkins all earned around $125 dollars a week (equivalent to around $3,000 today!), the only cast member earning less than the film's star was Terry, the female cairn terrier who played her dog Toto!

Another early blow to the production happened just weeks before filming when the glamorous American actress Gale Sondergaard—who had been cast as the Wicked Witch of the West—abandoned the production over disagreements as to how the witch should be portrayed. (According to one explanation, Sondergaard had been told that the witch was to be cool and cunning, like the Evil Queen in Snow White, and only later learned that she had been hired to play a green-skinned hag!) With Sondergaard gone, the producers had to work quickly to replace her and hired the eventual Wicked Witch, character actress Margaret Hamilton, just three days before shooting was to begin.

Once the filming was underway, however, the problems only went from bad to worse. Frank Morgan, the actor who played the titular Wizard, was a notorious heavy drinker who turned up to set the first day with a minibar full of cocktails in his suitcase. Then, the actor initially cast as the Tin Man, Buddy Ebsen, suffered such a severe reaction to inhaling the powdery aluminum makeup he had been coated in that he was sent to the hospital and had to withdraw from the film. (The actor who replaced him, Jack Haley, likewise suffered an eye infection from the aluminium on his face.) As for Hamilton, the green makeup she was coated in happened to be mildly flammable, and she received third-degree burns to her hands and face in a scene in which the witch is seen to vanish in a burst of flames and smoke. Filming was once again halted, and Hamilton had to take three months off to recover.

Of course despite all these problems (and a great many more like them!), *The Wizard of Oz* arrived in cinemas to rave reviews in August 1939. Unfortunately, the film's production had proved so problematic, however, that despite a multi-million dollar box office, it would take another decade for the film to turn a profit!

TOP 6 · FACTS
THE WIZARD OF OZ

- Famously, *The Wizard of Oz* is based on a book by the American author L. Frank Baum, but Baum in fact wrote an entire series of stories set in the world of Oz, of which *The Wonderful Wizard of Oz*, published in 1900, is just the first.

- According to his son's biography of him, having struggled to think up a name for the magical kingdom in which to set his stories, L. Frank Baum happened to glance up at the drawers of the file cabinet in his study where he wrote and saw that the last one was alphabetically labelled "O–Z." As a result, he named his fictional land "Oz."

- *The Wizard of Oz* was famously filmed in blazing Technicolor, and ultimately the set was bathed in rank after rank of red hot studio lights in order to make its colorful set come alive on screen. Unfortunately, the sheer number of lights required meant that temperatures on the set reportedly rose to over 100°F (38°C), leading to many of the cast and crew fainting during filming.

- The actor playing the Scarecrow in *The Wizard of Oz*, Ray Bolger, was required to wear a mask that was so thick and tight that he couldn't sweat through it. It took an hour to remove it after each day of filming, and he was left with permanent lines on his face.

- Terry the dog, who played Toto in *The Wizard of Oz*, turned out to be as great a Hollywood veteran as many of her co-stars and eventually starred in more than a dozen films.

- There were so many Munchkins in the movie that the film's clothing department had to create more than 1,000 costumes for a cast list of more than 600 performers.

Fill in the grid below so that each row of nine squares, each column of nine squares, and each smaller 3 x 3 set of nine squares contain the digits 1–9 once and only once.

There can be no duplicate digits in any row, column, or smaller square.

Can you complete the grid correctly?

	5	1	6			8	3		2
	8	3							5
		9	5		4	8	1	7
5		8			7		3	9
		2					7	
1	6			2	9			
	9	6	8				4	
2	7		9				5	8
8	1			4				3

Can you find your way through this maze from top to bottom?

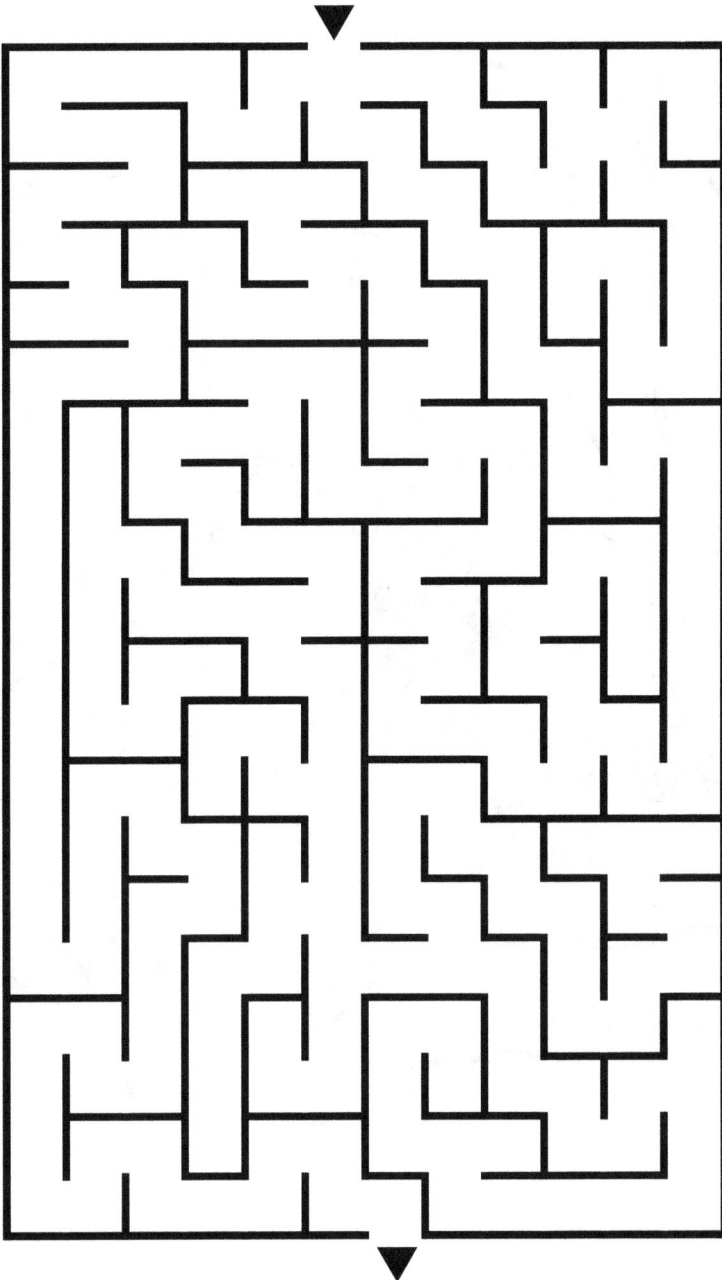

THE DISASTROUS CORONATION
OF WILLIAM THE CONQUEROR

William the Conqueror, Duke of Normandy, was the 11th-century Norman French nobleman who, in the autumn of 1066, launched an invasion of nearby England. Having defeated its only recently crowned king, the English earl Harold Godwinson, William secured the English throne for himself, and the dynasty that he began—known as the House of Normandy—would go on to rule medieval England for the next seven decades, 20 years of which was under King William himself.

William's predecessor, King Harold, was famously killed at the Battle of Hastings, near the south coast of England, on October 14, 1066, when an arrow fired by one of William's Norman troops struck him in the eye. (The entire affair, including Harold's gruesome death, is immortalized on the famous Bayeux Tapestry, which was commissioned to record William's remarkable victory in fabric in 1070.) Harold had only succeeded to the throne himself a little over 280 days earlier, on the death of medieval England's long-ruling king, Edward the Confessor. But with Harold now slain, and England now in possession of Norman France, William now had himself crowned, as only then could he rightfully call himself King William I of England. Unfortunately for him, however, ensuring that the English king's crown ended up on his head was a little easier said than done.

As news of Harold's death spread in the aftermath of the Battle of Hastings, William and his men had initially presumed that his new English subjects would merely accept the outcome, and his rule would face no further opposition. In reality, not many of the English people were quite so keen to accept a French king, and so several other smaller-scale battles and skirmishes continued to be played out across the southernmost quarter of England as William and his troops slowly closed in on London in the weeks, and eventually months, that followed. In the meantime, the English clergy and nobles quickly nominated their own choice of successor, Edgar, and began rallying support behind him in order to push William back and return the throne to English hands. Edgar's support was slow to form, however, and William used this time to take control of several key cities, including Dover, Winchester, and Canterbury.

By the time he and his men finally arrived in London, his rule was all but guaranteed, and he was crowned in Westminster Abbey on Christmas Day, 1066, a little over two months after his victory at Hastings. His coronation, however, was a debacle.

Aware that he was perhaps still not welcome among his new English subjects, William had guards positioned at various locations outside the abbey to prevent any potential protests or interruptions. Part of the ceremony itself, however, involved the English noblemen in attendance to loudly pledge their support for William's reign—a raucous announcement that the soldiers positioned outside Westminster Abby mistook for a Saxon riot. The troops responded to the apparent uprising by setting fire to houses and other buildings close to the abbey in an attempt to flush out any potential saboteurs or protestors (a situation which many of Williams' supporters reportedly used as an excuse for looting).

Back inside the abbey, meanwhile, the sound of the commotion outside and the smell of the smoke from the burning houses understandably caused panic, with much of the assembled congregation now convinced that there really was a riot. As a result, many of those in attendance fled the abbey in a frenzy, long before William's ceremony was completed. The king therefore had to be crowned in an all but deserted abbey, filled with the smoke from fires his own men had unnecessarily started.

It was an embarrassing and ignominious start to William's reign, and one that appears to have unnerved him: within a matter of days, William had demanded construction of a new castle in Westminster, ensuring that he could defend himself appropriately from any future challenges to his reign. The castle he built formed the foundations of what is now the Tower of London!

TOP 6 · FACTS
KINGS AND QUEENS

- William the Conqueror's funeral was even more farcical than his coronation. The room in which his body was kept was looted, and the king's naked and bloated body was left dumped on the floor. When the monks organizing the ceremony came to place him in his coffin, the king's stomach burst, apparently causing "an intolerable stench."

- William the Conqueror's son, William II, had just as unfortunate a time as his father. He died in mysterious circumstances while on a hunting expedition when a stray arrow fired by one of his companions struck him in the chest. Whether the king was the victim of a terrible accident or a plot by his younger brother Henry remains unknown to this day.

- King Edward II introduced a law in 1313 forbidding the wearing of suits of armor in the English Parliament. It remains in force to this day.

- England's king George I was born in Germany, spoke German as his first language, and spent so much of his life in Germany that his English court came to resent his rule. He even died while on another of his frequent trips home to Germany in 1727–and so was buried in Hanover, not London!

- Queen Elizabeth II was a qualified army mechanic. Having grown up in the Second World War, she played her part in England's war effort by enrolling in a military vehicle maintenance course at a training facility in Aldershot, near Windsor, and completed the course in April 1945.

- Charles III was 73 years old when he became king in 2022, making him the oldest crowned monarch in British history. He had been heir to throne for 70 years!

All 15 of these bathroom fixtures and fittings can be found in the grid below.

BASIN   **BATHTUB**   **BIDET**   **BOILER**

CABINET   **CISTERN**   **FAUCET**   **MIRROR**

RADIATOR   **SHOWER**   **SINK**   **SOAP DISPENSER**

TOILET   **TOWEL RAIL**   **WATER TANK**

```
U V E J S T O I L E T N C J K T J
S B C M R P Y X T G R K T X Q W K
T R A P I W M E W E S T H B U J X
R B Y T E R C K W M C E D Z M S L
E O Q S H U R O U Z F D B H E Z Z
S K E Q A T H O A M R I A H B Y D
N Q M F A S U J R D C B X B M I C
E C U K Z K B B J P X N D C U A S
P W Y H K O L L Z R K N I S B A I
S G Z F I N I X T W O S M I F V T
I P S L M K A W L M T T N G G W S
D X E T P A R T N E J E A U E G N
P R O N J X L D R K T D B I X V T
A A A L G O E N N E P P N R D R F
O B W U J V W I X H T R T E D A V
S W M M K O O K M B B A S I N L R
T D I F S Q T S G D N Q W P C L K
```

In what 8-letter English word will you find the string of consecutive letters below?

_ _ L K L O _ _

If you were to rotate the grid on the left here 90° counterclockwise, how would its network of shapes and symbols now appear? Draw the result in the grid on the right.

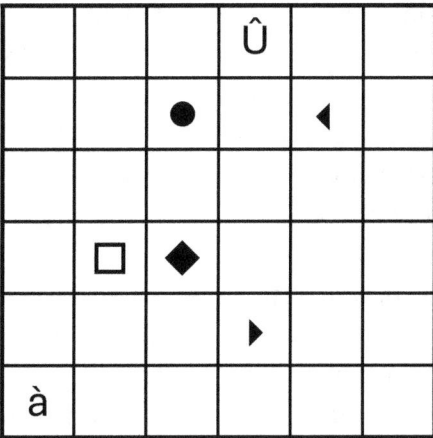

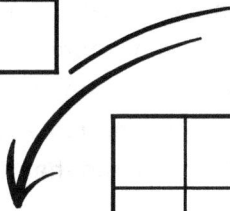

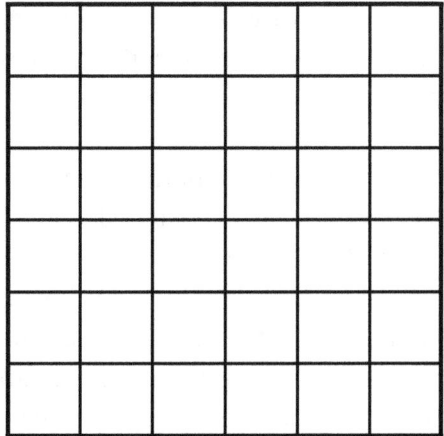

THE BEATLES FANS
WHO BELIEVE PAUL McCARTNEY
ISN'T WHO HE SAYS HE IS

T he Beatles are perhaps the most successful rock band in music history, with hundreds of millions of records sold around the world, a string of hit singles on both sides of the Atlantic, and a lasting impact on pop and rock music that continues to inspire and influence musicians today.

Formed in Liverpool in 1960, the band underwent several lineup changes in their early years, before the Fab Four—teenage best friends John Lennon and Paul McCartney, along with guitarist George Harrison and drummer Ringo Starr, the last to join the band—burst onto the music scene with their debut hit, "Love Me Do," in 1962. Over the years that followed, "Beatlemania," as the band's stratospheric popularity became known, caught on all over the world, and the group scored hit after hit in the 1960s with songs such as "She Loves You," "Help!," and "Penny Lane" and groundbreaking albums including *Revolver*, *Sgt. Pepper's Lonely Hearts Club Band*, and *Abbey Road*.

The Beatles went their separate ways in 1970, with all four members going on to achieve considerable solo success in the decades that followed. Beatles fans today, meanwhile, continue to be just as enamored with their music as they were at the height of their fame more than 50 years ago. But according to some—and according to one very old, and very persistent, urban myth—it was then, at the very height of the Beatles' fame in the mid 1960s, that something rather shocking happened to the band that was kept hidden from their fans, and continues to be kept secret to this day.

According to the rumors, it was back in 1966 that the Beatles' "original" Paul McCartney was tragically killed in a car accident. At that time, the band were at the pinnacle of their popularity and success, and so to maintain their career high—and to spare their legions of fans around the world from the doubtlessly immense outpouring of grief that would follow—the remaining three members decided to cover up the accident and employed none other than the British secret service, MI5, to assist them in the scheme.

Allegedly, the band quickly hired a Paul McCartney lookalike (and soundalike) who took Paul's place in the lineup as if nothing had happened—and it is this replacement, these conspiratorial fans believe, who continues to perform as Paul McCartney to this day.

As bizarre (and as understandably unlikely) as this conspiracy theory is, this rumor caused a furor in the mid 1960s, with some fans even claiming that all the band's music and album artwork from 1966 afterwards contains hints and clues proving that Paul was indeed dead. Play the Beatles' *Sgt. Pepper* album in reverse, these fans will say, and you'll hear John Lennon mumble "I buried Paul" at the end of "Strawberry Fields Forever" and the words "Paul is dead" played out in the background of "A Day in the Life." Look at the album cover in a mirror, moreover, and you might be able to read the words "X HE DIE" written on the central bass drum skin, not "Lonely Hearts." And on the band's penultimate 1969 album *Abbey Road*, the clues allegedly become even more clear, with "Paul is Dead" believers considering the album's famous cover art—featuring the four bandmembers walking across a pedestrian crossing on the eponymous road in central London—to be symbolic of a funeral procession. John, leading the way and dressed in white, represents a priest; Ringo, following in black, represents a mourner, or pallbearer; at the back of the group, George plays the part of a gravedigger, dressed in denim jeans and a loose denim shirt; while Paul, walking between George and Ringo in a simple gray suit, walks out of step with the others, symbolizing his demise, and is barefoot (because, in death, he doesn't need shoes).

So are these rumors true? Understandably, the band were always keen to dispel the story, with John Lennon once angrily dismissing it as "the most stupid rumour I've ever heard." As for (the real) Paul McCartney, he recently addressed the theory in a 2009 interview, long after the original furor died down. "I think the worst thing that happened," he told *Mojo* music magazine, "was that I could see people sort of looking at me more closely, [thinking] 'Were his ears always like that?'"

TOP 6 · FACTS
CELEBRITY CONSPIRACY THEORIES

- Pop superstar Avril Lavigne has also been subject to rumors that she died and has been replaced by a body double, who fans claim is named Melissa. Lavigne understandably laughed off the stories at the time, calling the rumor "dumb," but acknowledging that as far as celebrity conspiracies go, she "got a good one"!

- Elvis Presley has been the subject of numerous "sightings" all over the world ever since his death in 1977. Even on the afternoon of his death, on August 16, a man allegedly resembling him checked into a flight at Memphis Airport as Jon Burrows—an alias Elvis had long used to anonymously book hotels...

- Rumors that Vladimir Putin uses body doubles in public appearances have circulated since the 2000s, alongside reports that he is in poor health. Despite the rumors' popularity, no proof of his use of body doubles has ever been found.

- In the aftermath of the Second World War, rumors circulated that Hitler had not died in Berlin, but had fled to South America.

- When the *Titanic* sank in 1912, among the many passengers who lost their lives were three of the world's wealthiest businessmen: John Jacob Astor IV, Benjamin Guggenheim, and Isidor Straus. Their deaths led to rumors that the financier JP Morgan had arranged for the ship to be sunk as a means of seeing off competition and increasing his hold on the global financial markets.

- In 2024, Taylor Swift and her boyfriend, Kansas City Chiefs star Travis Kelce, were the subject of rumors claiming that the Super Bowl had been fixed that year in the Chiefs' favor in exchange for the couple endorsing Joe Biden in the presidential election. In the end, Biden dropped out of the presidential race, and his opponent, Donald Trump, won anyway!

All 15 of these B words connect together with one another in the grid. Can you find the right place for each one?

BACKCOMB	B-AND-B	BAOBAB	BATHBOMB
BATHTUB	BEDAUB	BENUMB	BICARB
BLURB	BOB	BOMB	BOOK CLUB
BREADCRUMB	BROKEN RIB	BULB	

How many squares are there in total in the figure below?

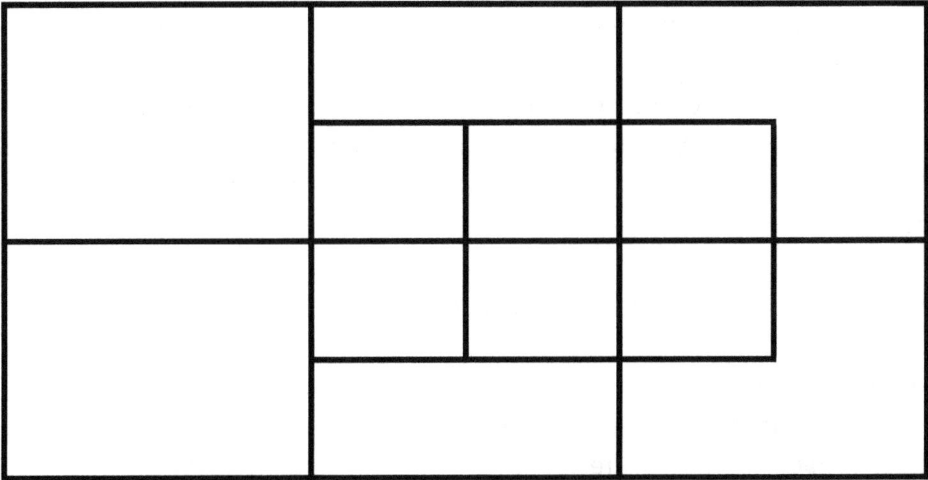

What two-word phrase is encoded in the figure below?

DIMENSIONAL
DIMENSIONAL
DIMENSIONAL

THE DOCTOR WHO WANTED TO BRING GEORGE WASHINGTON BACK TO LIFE

On December 14, 1799, America's first president, George Washington, finally succumbed to a devastating throat infection—now thought to have been an especially painful inflammation of the epiglottis—that had struck in the middle of the night just two days earlier. As his throat had continued to swell, both breathing and swallowing became difficult, and the former president's family called on a string of local doctors in an attempt to save his life.

The doctors administered a range of increasingly bizarre treatments, including purgative medicines, throat swabs, and even enemas. Fearing that the "humors" of his body must be in disarray, the president also had two-fifths of his blood let from his veins, leaving him even weaker than he was before. After 48 agonizing hours, President Washington politely requested his doctors leave him be, and, realizing that his time was coming to an end, asked instead that his secretary bring him his will. Having made a final request that his body not be interred until at least three days after his death (as Washington was reportedly terrified of being buried alive), the president reportedly uttered, "Do you understand me?" to his secretary Tobias Lear, before quietly slipping away with the words, "'Tis well."

As news of Washington's illness had spread in what proved to be his final hours, however, it eventually reached one of his friends, the physician Dr. William Thornton. Washington had been Thornton's benefactor for many years, and as a result, on hearing that his friend was deathly ill, the doctor decided to race to his bedside and join the string of physicians intending to offer their assistance and knowledge. Unfortunately, Thornton arrived too late to help, and the president had already been dead for several hours by the time he got to his home at Mount Vernon. But such was Thornton's determination to help—and his bizarre field of expertise—that he wasn't going to let a little thing like that stop him.

On discovering that Washington had already passed away, Thornton began explaining to the assembled doctors, staff, and grieving friends and family members at his Mount Vernon estate how he had been researching various techniques that could potentially re-animate his body and bring him back to life. Thornton wanted to take the president's body—which in the cold Virginia winter had already all but frozen solid—and gently warm it up, using blankets and water baths. Then, he wanted to open a passage into his lungs by performing an incision into his airways via a tracheotomy. And finally, to replace the blood that had been siphoned from his body, Thornton wanted to replace the president's most vital of fluids with that of a newborn lamb. "He died by the loss of blood and the want of air," Thornton later explained of his reasoning. "Restore these, with the heat that had subsequently been deducted, and ... there was no doubt in my mind that his restoration was possible."

Fortunately (or rather, unfortunately for Thornton) the assembled mourners and medical experts were none too keen to have America's founding president dealt with in this way after death and opted instead to leave him to rest. Thornton's bizarre experiments ultimately went unperformed, and Washington—in accordance to his wishes—was buried at his Mount Vernon home.

TOP 6 · FACTS
GEORGE WASHINGTON

- Although George Washington has gained a reputation today as a fearless and stoic soldier and general, in life he was pleasant natured and fun-loving and often hosted parties and cotilions at his Mount Vernon home that would go on into the early hours. He was also an avid reader, theatre-goer, and reportedly an excellent dancer!

- Despite popular history claiming his false teeth were made of wood, Washington's dentures were actually a mixture of gold, ivory, human teeth, and animal bone!

- Before he entered the military and later politics, Washington's first job was as a surveyor. He enrolled on his first surveying expedition into the Virginia wilderness in 1748 when he was just 16 years old.

- The only time Washington ever left mainland America was to travel to Barbados in 1751 with his half-brother, Lawrence, who had been advised to spend time in the tropics to improve his health. While he was there, George contracted smallpox and fell deathly ill himself!

- After retiring from politics, Washington opened a distillery and began brewing his own whiskey. George Washington's Rye Whiskey is now the official state spirit of Virginia.

- Although a born-and-bred American, Washington was made an honorary citizen of France in 1792 in response to his vocal support for the French Revolution.

9

The answer to each clue in this grid begins in the corresponding numbered square. The last letter of one answer is the first letter of the next.

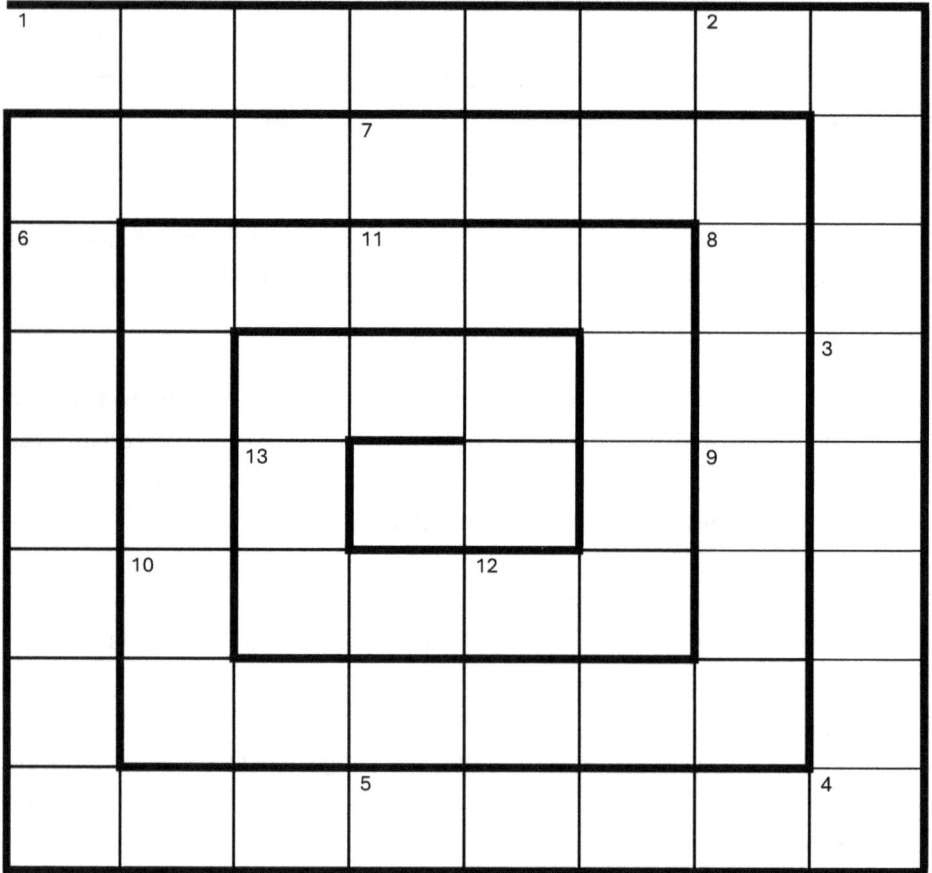

1						2	
			7				
6			11		8		
							3
		13			9		
	10			12			
		5				4	

1. Proof of purchase

2. ___ New Roman, typeface

3. Aroma

4. Italian city

5. Compass point opposite southwest

6. Goblin under a bridge

7. Organ that produces digestive bile

8. Scarlet, for example

9. Vanish

10. Haphazard

11. Mechanical device

12. Terminates

13. Yarn

What direction would you have to turn gear A in order for gear B to rotate clockwise?

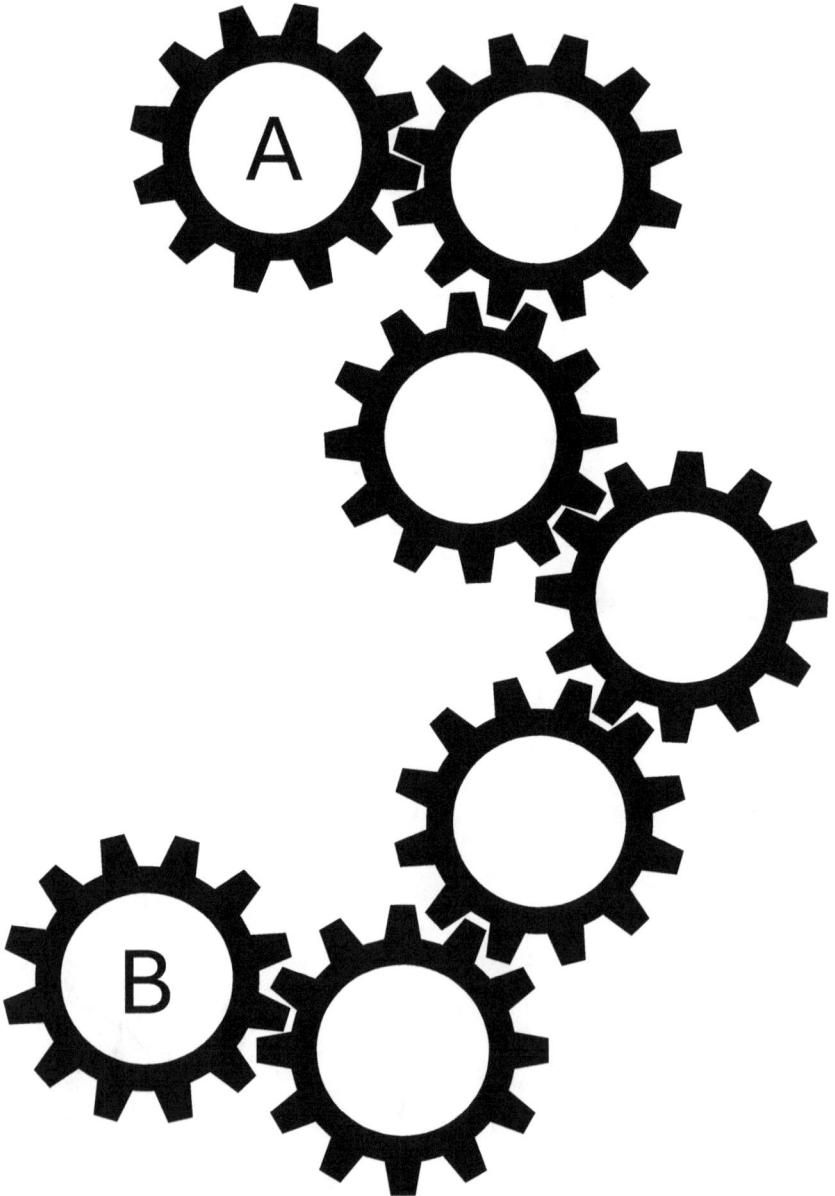

THAT TIME A TOP HAT
CAUSED A RIOT

From early 2000s bootcut jeans to 80s-style crimped hair and legwarmers, all manner of fads and fashions have fallen in and out of favor over the decades. Go back in time far enough, in fact, and even the oldest and most traditional fashions would doubtless have one day been considered new, daring, and bizarre. And that is perhaps no more true than with one of the most standard and traditional of fashion accessories—the gentleman's top hat.

According to newspaper reports from the late 19th century, the world's first top hat was debuted in London in 1797 by a local gentleman and haberdasher named John Hetherington. Having apparently conceived of, designed, and finally made a tall, cylindrical, silk-covered black hat, Hetherington stepped out onto the streets of The Strand in Westminster, central London, on January 16 and instantly caused a considerable commotion.

"John Hetherington, haberdasher of the Strand," read one newspaper report, "was arraigned before the Lord Mayor yesterday, on a charge of breach of the peace and inciting to riot." For his apparent crimes, Hetherington was "required to give bonds in the sum of £500"—an astronomical figure equivalent to over £50,000 ($63,000) today!—for daring to have appeared outside "upon the public highway, wearing upon his head what he called a silk hat."

The report goes on to describe that Hetherington's remarkable headwear was "a tall structure" with "a shiny lustre," which was so remarkable in size and shape that, according to descriptions at the time, it must have been intentionally designed and "calculated to frighten timid people." In fact, it is recorded that "several women fainted at the unusual sight, while children screamed, dogs yelped, and a younger son of Cordwainer Thomas … was thrown down by the crowd which had collected and had his right arm broken" as he returned from a trip to a local chandler's shop. "For these reasons, the defendant was seized by the guards, and taken to the Lord Mayor."

Ever since this story was circulated in the Victorian press, the so-called Top Hat Riot of 1797 has since become the stuff of legend and a perfect example of the forever daring and bizarre nature of the latest fashions. Unfortunately, "legend" may well be the appropriate word here, however, as there are many historians and fashion writers alike who now claim that this somewhat remarkable story is little more than an urban myth. Despite its appearance in the press, the true details of John Hetherington's brush with the law have never been proven, and there is no surviving evidence of his haberdashery business in London, his address on the Strand, nor of the riot he apparently caused simply by stepping outside wearing a top hat. Whether true or not, however, the story remains popular—even if the hat itself has not, having long ago ceased to become an everyday item of clothing for the average gentleman!

TOP 6 · FACTS
WEIRD FASHIONS

- There was a fashion among Victorian women for having the minutest waist possible. Many achieved this by wearing tight corsets and boddices under their clothing—but another method was to grossly exaggerate the size of their skirts, below the waist, so that the top half of their bodies appeared smaller in comparison. As a result, women often wore networks of bone-like struts, known as crinolines, beneath their skirts, making them stick out far beyond their legs and body!

- The Egyptians, Greeks, and Romans used a substance called *kohl* as an eye shadow and eyeliner. It was made by crushing a mineral containing a metal called antimony, but samples tested today have been shown to contain a far higher quantity of lead, making them toxic!

- Some African tribes have a fashion for "lip plates," in which a woman's lower lip is pierced and then gradually expanded by placing ever larger wooden disks into the hole. Some women of Ethiopia's Suri tribe wear disks as wide as their face!

- In 16th century Europe, high-society women wore bizarre tapered, platform-style shoes, known as chopines, which were seen as a symbol of high status (while lifting the wearer far above the dirt and grime of the streets!). Although highly precarious and difficult to walk in, some chopines were more than 20 inches tall!

- In the mid 1910s, American women endured a (thankfully brief) trend known as the hobble skirt—a style of close-fitting skirt that tapered to the ankle, allowing the wearer to take only tiny steps! An antidote to the grand gowns and petticoats of the Victorian era, the Edwardian hobble skirt proved popular for only a brief time, doubtless due to the near endless stream of newspaper reports of women falling and suffering ankle injuries while wearing them!

- In Elizabethan times there was a fashion for padded clothing, which was used to exaggerate everything from the size of women's chests to men's upper arms and calves. The padding was known as bombast and remained popular until the mid 1600s.

Can you match the famous sportspeople on the left to their sports on the right?

The first has been filled in to get you started.

Rafael Nadal	**American football**
Travis Kelce	**Basketball**
Sebastian Vettel	**Gymnastics**
Simone Biles	**Tennis**
Michael Phelps	**Baseball**
Nikola Jokić	**Soccer**
Aaron Judge	**Motor racing**
Lionel Messi	**Swimming**

Rafael Nadal — Tennis

Each of the letters in the quotation below has been swapped for another.
Can you decode the message?

"NCU V QY UX LGQDH VL MHPZ,

"_H_ _ A_ __ _T___ _S __R_,

MHPZ IVOOHPHXG GU NCU V QY

V___ ___F___N_ __ __O _ __

VX PHQF FVOH." - SHZUXJH

__ ___L _I__." - _EY____

What two-word phrase is encoded in the figure below?

CCCCCCC

THE VOLCANO THAT FILLED A TOWN WITH SNAKES

History is peppered with extraordinary stories of natural disasters, from the earthquake that destroyed the famous Lighthouse at Alexandria (one of the Seven Wonders of the Ancient World) to the eruption of the Krakatoa volcano, in western Indonesia, which was so enormous that it briefly altered the climate of the entire world! In 1902, however, another devastating volcanic eruption struck the Caribbean island of Martinique, 400 miles southeast of Puerto Rico.

Like many of the islands in the Caribbean's Lesser Antilles chain—including Barbados, Antigua, St. Lucia, and Trinidad—Martinique is a mountainous island whose landscape is dominated by four gigantic peaks: Pitons du Carbet, Morne Jacob, Mount Pelée, and Piton Conil. All four of these peaks rise to more than 1,000 m (3,200 ft) above sea level, with the tallest, Mount Pelée, standing a full 1,397 m (4,583 ft) tall—making it quite a sight on an island only eighteen times larger than Manhattan!

Alongside being the island's highest peak, however, Mount Pelée is not just an ordinary mountain. In fact, it is an active volcano, whose last major eruption in 1902 was almost indescribably devastating. Following several days of rumbles and tremors, shortly after 8 o'clock in the morning on May 8, the volcano finally blew its top in an immense explosion that sent a wave of scorching gas, steam, and mud down its slopes. In the way was the town of Saint-Pierre—a beautiful bay area port known as the Paris of the "Paris of the West Indies"—which was almost instantaneously flattened. A staggering 30,000 people were killed in a disaster that unfolded inside just three minutes; according to some reports, there was just one survivor in the town of Saint-Pierre, who just so happened to be a prisoner housed far out of harm's way in a cell at the center of the town's police station. But although the eruption of Mount Pelée that morning proved to be the end of the town, in the days leading up to it the townspeople had to deal with a somewhat unexpected (and just as horrifying) spectacle.

It is often said that animals and birds can interpret an oncoming natural disaster far better than we humans can—and the Mount Pelée disaster was no different. In the hours and days leading up to the eruption, minor tremors and rumbles around the volcano began disturbing the wildlife. And just like the flow of gas and mud that would eventually follow it, the creatures themselves fled down the mountainside and headed directly for the town.

First came the insects. For days, Saint-Pierre was infested with biting ants, spiders, and centipedes, which began moving down the rainforest-covered mountain and straight into the homes and roads of the town. Once that first wave was over, however, it was followed by a far more disturbing one as hundreds of venomous snakes slithered their way down the slopes and into the town and the surrounding countryside. Hundreds of livestock were bitten and killed, as were around 50 local residents who quickly succumbed to the venom of 6ft-long pit vipers; there were so many snakes that, according to reports, soldiers were sent out into the streets to shoot the snakes to death on sight in an effort to protect the local people.

As unpleasant as the bugs, centipedes, and snakes were, of course, in the end all efforts to protect the town and its people were futile—making Mount Pelée yet another reminder that we humans are forever at the mercy of the world in which we live.

TOP 6 · FACTS
VOLCANOES

- Volcanoes take their name from the Roman god Vulcan, who was depicted as a blacksmith who controlled the fires of the earth.

- Volcanoes don't just throw out molten rock and gas when they explode. In fact, the ash and other debris that some volcanoes produce is often full of rich mineral deposits, making the land around volcanic slopes highly fertile and suitable for agriculture. As a result, it has been estimated that nearly half a billion people worldwide willingly live inside the danger zone of active volcanoes—which could erupt at any moment!

- When the Indonesian volcano of Krakatoa erupted in 1883, it produced an explosion so loud that it could be heard more than 2,000 miles away in Australia!

- Propelled by the explosion and drawn down the mountainsides by gravity, the material ejected from a volcano can travel at extraordinary speeds. A so-called pyroclastic flow—a vast, scorching hot cloud of steam, rock, dust, ash, and other volcanic particles—can travel at 200 mph!

- The world's largest active volcano is Mauna Loa in Hawaii. Rising to more than 13,681 feet (4,170 m) above sea level, the vast round peak is so large that it takes up half of the entire island of Hawai'i!

- There are over 160 volcanoes in the United States, making it the most volcanic country on the planet. However, barely 60 of these peaks have shown any volcanic activity in the last 200 years; the most volcanically active country on the planet is in fact Indonesia, where 59 different volcanoes have erupted since 1950!

- 13 -
WORD JUMBLE

In each of the boxes below, the letters from two words that fit the corresponding subject category have been muddled up together. Can you unjumble them? The first has been filled in for you to get you started.

Albany	**1. US "New" state capitals** **AAAABEFLNNSTY**	*Santa Fe*
	2. Taylor Swift albums **EEFKLLLOOORRV**	
	3. Planets **EEIJNPRSTUUV**	
	4. Yellow fruits **AAABELMNNNO**	
	5. You put them up in the rain **ABDEHLLMOORU**	
	6. Things on a bed **ABEIKLLNQTTU**	

The eight single-digit numbers below have been removed from this magic square.

Replace the numbers in the grid so that the four boxes on each row and in each column total 39.

2 3 4 5 6 7 8 9

	12	16	
15			13
	18	10	
11			17

A HAUNTING AT THE WHITE HOUSE

Almost every old house or castle the world over will have some local myth about the ghost (or ghosts, as the case may be!) that supposedly haunt it. And as President Harry Truman found to his surprise in 1946, the White House is apparently no different.

The story begins on a warm evening early in the September of 1946. President Truman's wife, Bess, was staying out of town, and so having worked alone all day in his office at the White House, the president retired to bed alone at around 9 o'clock. The night was hot, and unfortunately the president's bedroom was apparently plagued with mosquitos, so he had already endured a restless and uncomfortable night's sleep when, at around 4 o'clock in the morning, he was suddenly awoken by a series of three distinct knocks on his bed chamber door. Given the importance of his job, of course, the president understandably leapt from his bed to answer the door, doubtless fearing that something serious had happened that required his urgent attention. Having pulled on his bathrobe and opened the door, however, he found the corridor outside to be completely empty. Puzzled, President Truman walked out of his bedroom and into the hall, and from there into the adjoining rooms that were usually used by his family; to his surprise and confusion, the entire area was deserted.

Perhaps presuming that there might have been a draft—or else perhaps that thumps or footsteps from somewhere else in the White House might have been making the corridor doors creak and judder—President Truman retrieved his keys and locked some of the doors to the adjoining rooms before promptly returning to bed, thinking no more of it. But almost as soon as he was back under the covers, he heard another sound—this time, a series of footsteps coming not from the corridor, but from one of the bedrooms he had just peeked into. He knew the rooms were empty, and so again he leapt from his bed and back out into the hall; the room in which he had heard the footsteps was one of the few whose door he had left open, but again when he looked inside, he found no one. This entire spooky episode was recorded by President Truman himself in a letter written to his wife a day or two later, on September 9, 1942. "At four o'clock I was awakened by three distinct knocks on my bedroom door," he wrote. "Went out and looked up and down the hall, looked into your room and Margie's [his daughter Margaret]. Still no one. Went back to bed after locking the doors and there were footsteps in your room, whose door I'd left open. Jumped and looked and no one there!"

For the president, there was just one possible conclusion. "The damned place is haunted, sure as shootin'," he wrote to Bess. "Secret service said not even a watchman was up here at that hour. You and Margie had better come back and protect me before some of these ghosts carry me off!"

TOP 6 · FACTS
GHOSTS AND HAUNTINGS

- The New Amsterdam Theater in New York is said to be haunted by a Broadway chorus girl named Olive Thomas, who took her own life in 1920 after a whirlwind romance came to an end. According to legend, Olive's ghost, dressed in a green gown, can be seen walking the halls and corridors of the theater, still clutching the empty bottle of mercury bichloride medicine that she took to end her life.

- Broadway's Lyceum Theatre is said to be haunted by the ghost of the famous choreographer Bob Fosse.

- Some Parisians will tell you that the Louvre is haunted by the ghost of an Egyptian mummy, named Belphegor, who is housed there. Although it is true that the Louvre has a mummy (as well as its fair share of ghosts!), this tale is based on a 1927 novel called *Belphégor*, which told the story of a criminal who disguises himself as a ghost to rob the museum.

- Just as the White House has its ghost, so too does Britain's 10 Downing Street, which is supposedly home to a specter called the Lady in White. Her ghost is said to walk around the house's State Dining Room, where her footsteps and the swishing of her taffeta dress can sometimes be heard.

- The late Queen Elizabeth II and her sister Margaret claimed to have seen the ghost of Elizabeth I walking through the library of Windsor Castle.

- Hampton Court Palace in London is said to be one of the royal family's most haunted properties. One of Henry VIII's more favored residences, it is home to the ghost of his wife Catherine Howard, who was beheaded in 1542. Reportedly, her ghost can be seen reliving the moment of her arrest, running and screaming through the palace's corridors.

- 15 -

How quickly can you solve this crossword?

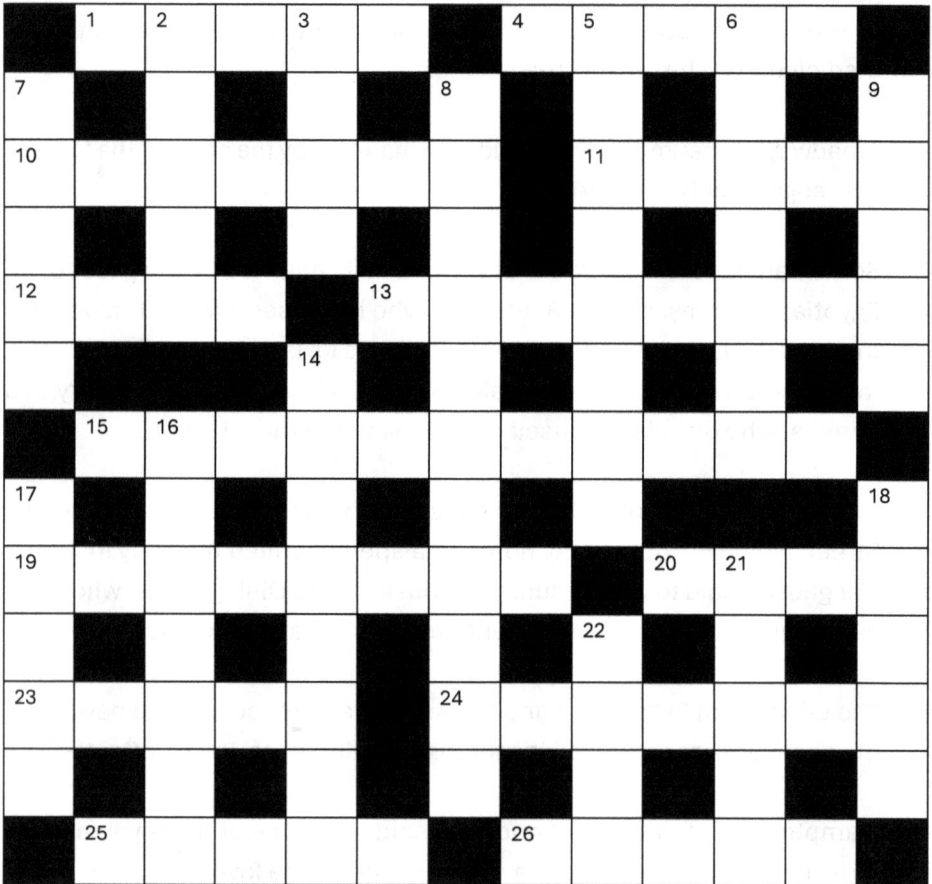

ACROSS

1. Fumes from a fire
4. Posed a question
10. Retaliation
11. Very small
12. Profound
13. Come closer to
15. European country
19. Power
20. As well
23. Proof you were elsewhere at the time of a crime
24. Recuperate
25. Boasts
26. Not tight

DOWN

2. Film
3. Male monarch
5. First day of the weekend
6. Green gem
7. Group of lions
8. Measure of heat
9. Legends
14. Mulling over
16. Previously
17. Regular order
18. Apologetic
21. Adores
22. Reverberate

The 16 words and phrases in the grid below can be arranged into four connected groups of four—that is, with each set of four answers having something in common.

Can you work out the connections? Be careful, though—some answers might belong in more than one group, but there is only one overall solution!

Jackdaw	Knight	Lawn	Queen
Wrath	Flamingo	Magpie	Pterodactyl
Sundial	Bishop	Jay	Pond
Rook	Gnome	Raven	Pawn

THE STORY OF THE IGUANODON'S THUMB

Nowadays, we're all familiar with the idea that gigantic dinosaurs once roamed the Earth. We have movies and television documentaries about them, and dinosaur-mad kids can be kept entertained with games, soft toys, jigsaw puzzles, and all manner of other entertainment featuring pictures and models of enormous fearsome reptiles.

Two centuries ago, however, no one knew that dinosaurs had ever even existed—and it wasn't until 1824 that an English naturalist named William Buckland happened to stumble across a gigantic, fossilized jawbone in a slate quarry not far from the city of Oxford.

Giant bones like this had been found before, but people had always assumed them to be those of living creatures. Buckland, however, knew from this bone's appearance that it must have belonged to some manner of reptilian creature, unlike any alive in England today—or, for that matter, living anywhere else on Earth. He presented his findings to the Geological Society of London and announced that he had found the remains of what he presumed to be an ancient gigantic reptile, which he called Megalosaurus—a name meaning "great lizard." Buckland's discovery was the first of its kind and soon unlocked a frenzy of dinosaur hunting in Victorian England. Before long, more and more enormous fossilized bones were being discovered in quarries, stone pits, embedded in cliff faces, and along rocky coastlines all around the world, each one belonging to a different species of ancient animal. A few years later, in 1841, one of Buckland's colleagues, Richard Owen, named these ancient creatures Dinosauria, and we have known them as dinosaurs—literally "terrible lizards"—ever since.

After two centuries of research and discovery, however, we know an awful lot more about the dinosaurs' world than Buckland, Owen, and the other dinosaur hunters of the 19th century could ever have imagined. All that they had to go on was a rather limited knowledge of animals and natural history, and as a result many of their early theories about the appearance and behavior of dinosaurs were not quite right. And one famous example of just how wrong they could be happened just a year after Buckland's discovery, in 1825.

An English geologist named Gideon Mantell had recently discovered a series of bones he believed belonged to some manner of gigantic iguana-like lizard. He named the creature Iguanodon and began doing his best to piece the skeleton back together. Amid the pile of bones he had unearthed, however, was a small cone-shaped bone, which—based on the appearance of iguanas today—Mantell believed must be a nose horn, rather like that of a rhinoceros. All early replicas of Iguanodon dinosaurs, ultimately, came to depict the creatures as having a small bony horn on their snout.

Scientists continued to believe that Iguanodons had a horn on their nose for the next 50 years, until a series of more complete Iguanodon skeletons were unearthed in rural Belgium. Incredibly, these remains proved without doubt that this small conical bone was not actually a horn, but a thumb bone, which the ancient plant-eating creatures perhaps used to grasp grasses, branches, and trees—or, according to another theory, as a means of defending itself!

TOP 6 · FACTS
DINOSAURS

- The first dinosaurs emerged in the Triassic period, around 250 million years ago.

- In total, dinosaurs roamed the Earth during three distinct periods of ancient history—the Triassic, the Jurassic, and the Cretaceous—covering around 245 million years in all, until their disappearance around 65 million years ago. Not all dinosaurs lived at the same time, however. The vast length of time across which the dinosaurs inhabited the Earth means that some were alive closer in time to today than the beginning of the dinosaur age!

- To date, around 700 distinct dinosaur species have been discovered, with remains unearthed on all seven of the Earth's continents—including Antarctica!

- Although everything we know about dinosaurs tends to come from their bones, their eggs, teeth, footprints, and even droppings have all been unearthed by paleontologists!

- The largest dinosaurs—and the largest land animals ever to have lived on the Earth—are known as the Titanosaurs. These long-necked, plant-eating dinosaurs lived toward the end of the Cretaceous Period, around 145–165 million years ago, with an individual Titanosaur species called Dreadnoughtus believed to be the largest of all: it was around 85 ft (26 m) long and would have weighed about 65 tons!

- At the other end of the scale, one of the smallest dinosaurs ever discovered was Micropachycephalosaurus (meaning "little thick-headed lizard"!). Despite its long name, this tiny dinosaur was barely a meter long and would have stood only around a foot (30 cm) tall.

Fill in the grid below so that each row of nine squares, each column of nine squares, and each smaller 3 x 3 set of nine squares contain the digits 1–9 once and only once.

There can be no duplicate digits in any row, column, or smaller square.

Can you complete the grid correctly?

4	5	6	2	9	3			1
			4	6				2
3		9	8	1		5	4	
6	1		7	4	2			9
8	9		6	5	1	2		4
	7		9	3		6		
9				8			2	
	4			7	6	9	5	
5			1	2	9	4		7

What three-word phrase is pictured below?

DRIVE

All the vowels—A, E, I, O and U—have been removed from this 5-by-5 mini crossword. Can you replace them?

T		L		D
H	■	L	■	
R			C	T
	■	M	■	T
B	R		V	

THE MADMAN WHO HELPED WRITE THE OXFORD ENGLISH DICTIONARY

Containing more than 600,000 entries, the *Oxford English Dictionary* is one of the world's biggest, most respected, and most impressive publications. But perhaps understandably for a such a gigantic work of literature, compiling the dictionary was not an easy task and eventually took almost 80 years to complete—all with the help of a rather unlikely individual.

It was way back in the 1850s that an academic organization called the London Philological Society decided to embark upon compiling and writing a new definitive English dictionary. No similar work had been produced in England for almost a century, and with new research and technologies now at their disposal, the society members decided that this was the right time to update their understanding of our language.

The project initially had an uneasy start, with much of the early work of collecting words and literary quotations—all of which were handwritten on hundreds of thousands of individual slips of paper—stalling when the dictionary's first editor died unexpectedly of tuberculosis at the age of just 30. After another 20 years of progress under a new editor, in 1878 the dictionary (along with two tons of alphabetized paper slips!) was handed over to a Scottish schoolteacher named James Murray, who remained in charge for the next four decades.

Murray knew that in order for the dictionary to be truly representative of the full English language, it needed to have input from as many people as possible. As a result, he cleverly decided to open up the process of writing the dictionary to the public and played advertisements in newspapers requesting that people send him and his team as many examples of how words are used—and have been used in the past—to him at his offices. Hundreds of people responded to Murray's request, and over the years that followed the number of paper slips from which the dictionary was compiled grew enormously. One of the people who assisted Murray the most in his work was an American-born man living in London, named Dr. William Chester Minor.

W.C. Minor was born in Connecticut in 1834 and had worked as an army surgeon during the American Civil War. His experiences on the battlefield had unfortunately stayed with him, and Minor gradually began to lose his mind in the years afterwards. In an effort to escape his growing madness, Minor relocated to England in 1871—but a year later, in a fit of paranoia, he shot and killed a man in central London, having wrongly believed him to be a thief. Murray was arrested, but his obviously worsening mental state led to him being sent to Broadmoor, an asylum for the criminally insane, in Berkshire on the outskirts of London.

It was while incarcerated at Broadmoor that Minor saw Murray's request for written evidence of English words and began a twenty-year obsession with aiding in Murray's work. Despite being in prison, Minor had access to a library of books and, as an avid reader, was able to provide Murray with quotations and evidence of many thousands of individual words. By the time the first volumes of the Oxford English Dictionary were finally released to the public in 1880s and 90s, Murray estimated that Minor's contributions had provided over four centuries worth of the written evidence they contained.

Despite his stellar work—and despite numerous petitions from Murray to the government of the time—Minor remained in prison until 1910, when he was 75 years old. He died at home a decade later in 1920. As for Murray, sadly he did not live to see his work completed and died in 1915 at the age of 78; the final volume of the *Oxford English Dictionary*, covering the letters V to Z, was published after his death, in 1928.

TOP 6 · FACTS
WORDS AND DICTIONARIES

- The longest word in a standard English dictionary is typically *pneumonoultramicroscopicsilicovolcanoconiosis*—the name of a kind of lung disease caused by inhaling silica dust. It has 45 letters.

- If technical and chemical terms are permitted, however, the longest known possible word in the English language is the full chemical name of a muscular protein known as titin. The name—which begins *methionylthreonylthreonylglutaminylalanylprolylthreonylphenylalanyl...*—in full contains 189,819 letters!

- A pangram is a word or sentence that contains every letter of the alphabet at least once. The most famous example is "The quick brown fox jumps over the lazy dog," which was invented in the late 1880s as a handwriting (and later typing) exercise.

- One of the shortest known pangrams is "Waltz, bad nymph, for quick jigs vex," which contains just 28 letters (with only the A and I repeated!).

- Samuel Johnson's *Dictionary of the English Language*, published in 1755, was the definitive guide to the language at the time. As one of the most famous wits of his day, Johnson took the opportunity to fill his dictionary with jokes and fairly unserious definitions. Luggage, for instance, Johnson defined as "anything of more bulk than value." Lunch was "as much food as one's hand can hold." And a lizard was "an animal resembling a serpent, with legs added to it."

- A word that can be made from the letters of another word is called an anagram. Only one of the days of the week has an anagram in English: Monday can be rearranged to spell dynamo!

Take a peek inside the bathroom cabinet with this wordsearch.

ANTISEPTIC **BANDAGES** **COTTONBALLS**
EYEDROPS **MAKEUP** **NAILCLIPPERS**
OINTMENT **PAINKILLERS** **PLASTERS**
Q-TIPS **SCISSORS** **SKIN CREAM**
TISSUES **TOOTHBRUSH** **TOOTHPASTE**

```
N  D  B  T  U  D  I  Z  U  O  E  L  M  V  C  N  R
S  R  E  P  P  I  L  C  L  I  A  N  A  T  O  S  X
A  X  P  X  B  A  F  G  F  K  D  F  E  I  T  E  H
H  K  G  M  D  Z  O  W  Q  A  R  I  R  S  T  V  D
U  P  K  E  Q  A  S  P  I  T  Q  W  C  S  O  S  C
T  O  O  T  H  B  R  U  S  H  S  S  N  U  N  R  I
W  O  S  P  O  R  D  E  Y  E  R  T  I  E  B  E  T
H  M  I  J  A  E  Z  Y  G  O  A  S  K  S  A  L  P
Y  Z  D  R  S  K  T  A  S  X  T  I  S  U  L  L  E
R  Y  Q  K  B  P  D  S  O  P  Q  Y  X  K  L  I  S
K  C  I  Y  G  N  I  I  A  P  L  V  K  T  S  K  I
Y  U  S  G  A  C  N  J  U  P  Y  A  F  M  L  N  T
U  I  R  B  S  T  W  E  K  L  H  Q  S  C  N  I  N
N  P  K  G  M  Y  K  C  J  O  G  T  K  T  G  A  A
O  E  Y  E  M  A  G  T  U  H  L  B  O  Y  E  P  P
G  Z  N  N  M  S  H  K  X  B  T  G  W  O  T  R  N
M  T  K  X  Y  I  E  T  X  E  G  A  E  N  T  F  S
```

What is the next letter in each of these sequences?

F M A M J ?

A C F J O ?

E O E R E ?

Each of the 5-letter words below is missing its middle letter. Place those missing letters in the corresponding spaces in the grid, and a 7-letter word will be revealed reading down the central column. Watch out, though—there might be more than one possible missing letter for some words, but there is only one possible solution.

▼

F	R		T	H
S	T		F	F
W	A		E	R
F	U		S	Y
C	L		M	B
T	O		A	Y
C	H		C	K

CHARLES JOUGHIN, THE LAST SURVIVOR TO LEAVE THE *TITANIC*

2 hours and 40 minutes after it struck an iceberg in the freezing waters of the north Atlantic Ocean early in the morning of April 15, 1912, the RMS *Titanic* finally disappeared beneath the surface of the sea. It has long been said that 34-year-old crewmate Charles Joughin was the last person to leave the ship and one of the few passengers who survived long enough in the water to be rescued and survive the entire ordeal. But as remarkable as Joughin's tale is, what is perhaps even more unusual is the somewhat unlikely twist of fate that happened to keep him alive.

Joughin was employed as the head baker of the *Titanic*. His job was to supply its passengers with fresh bread, pastries, and cakes for the entirety of their trip from Europe to America. After it hit the iceberg, Joughin used his position to hand out bread and biscuits to passengers in the ship's lifeboats to keep them fed and helped many of the women and children who were the first to leave the ship to find places in the boats themselves. As the night wore on and the fate of the *Titanic* became clear, Joughin was one of the many crew members who began tossing deck chairs and other wooden items over the side of the ship to act as makeshift floatation devices for those unlucky enough to find themselves without a space in the lifeboats. Finally, he headed to the very rear of the ship in an effort to delay his own inevitable descent into the ocean and was said by many eyewitnesses to have been the very last person visible above the waves on the hull as the ship went down.

Throughout this long ordeal, however, Joughin was taking discreet nips from a hipflask of whiskey that he reportedly had in his pocket—likely as both an antidote to the frigid temperatures and as a means of steeling himself and giving himself a much-needed dose of Dutch courage. But as Joughin eventually ended up in the 18°F (–2°C) waters of the Atlantic Ocean that night, it is more than possible that the alcohol in his system may well have been what allowed him to survive more than two hours treading water before being rescued by the nearby Carpathia in the early hours of the morning.

Admittedly, alcohol is not generally a good (nor particularly healthy) way of maintaining body heat: in scientific terms, it causes a bodily process called vasodilation, in which the blood vessels in the skin open, increasing blood flow and thereby accelerating heat loss. In such cold conditions as the *Titanic* found itself that night, drinking whiskey might well have increased Joughin's likelihood of developing hypothermia—a dangerous and potentially deadly decrease in body temperature.

When people find themselves submerged in cold water, however, they rarely survive long enough to succumb to hypothermia. Instead, the shock of the cold often causes them to breathe more rapidly and raggedly, increasing a risk of drowning, while the sudden cold constricts the blood vessels, causing an increase in blood pressure, and ultimately, in some instances, triggering a cardiac arrest. While it is likely that many of the *Titanic*'s other passengers fell victim to this so-called deadly "cold shock response," the alcohol in Joughin's system may well have reduced the impact of the shock on his body, while its intoxicating effects allowed him to remain calm enough to control his breathing and see out the next few hours in the water.

Quite how much whiskey Joughin had in his system as the *Titanic* went down is unclear, but it is certainly likely that however much he had drank, it was this—along with his own clear-headedness and resolve—that saved his life that night.

TOP 6 · FACTS
THE *TITANIC*

- The *Titanic*'s proper name was the RMS *Titanic*. That's because as well as being a passenger liner, it was a postal vessel equipped for carrying transatlantic mail; the letters RMS stand for Royal Mail Ship.

- The *Titanic* had just 20 lifeboats, despite there being over 2,000 people on board. The ship's designer, Alexander Carlisle, had initially planned for 48, but that number was reduced as it was worried the lifeboats would clutter the upper-class decks. Even the number Carlisle had suggested was far from the total number of lifeboats the ship had room for: there was enough space on deck for 64 lifeboats, which could have carried well over 3,000 people to safety.

- Although first-class passengers were given preferential treatment, some 40% of them died in the disaster (mostly due to the lifeboats being filled with women and children first). Nonetheless, three-quarters of third-class passengers died in the sinking, along with almost two-thirds of those in second class.

- Although around 1,500 people died on the *Titanic*, 3 in 10 of the ship's total number of passengers and crew survived. Had the ship's lifeboats been filled to capacity, however, more than half of those on board could have been saved.

- When she died in 2009 at the age of 97, Millvina Dean was the longest-lived survivor of the *Titanic*; she was just 9 months old when the ship sank in 1912.

- By far the largest ship in the world at the time, the *Titanic* was 880 ft long and 92 ft wide and had a gross tonnage (weight) of over 46,000 tons. The world's largest ship today, however, is the Royal Caribbean's Icon of the Seas. Launched in 2022, it is almost 1,200 ft long and 160 ft wide and has a gross tonnage of almost a quarter of a million tons!

The L words and phrases listed below all connect together in the grid.
Can you work out where each one goes?

LANDFILL	**LATITUDINAL**	**LAWFUL**	**LENTIL**
LEG-PULL	**LIBEL**	**LICENSED TO KILL**	**LIVERPOOL**
LOGICAL	**LOL**	**LOST SOUL**	**LOVERS' QUARREL**
LOW-CAL	**LOYAL**	**LULL**	

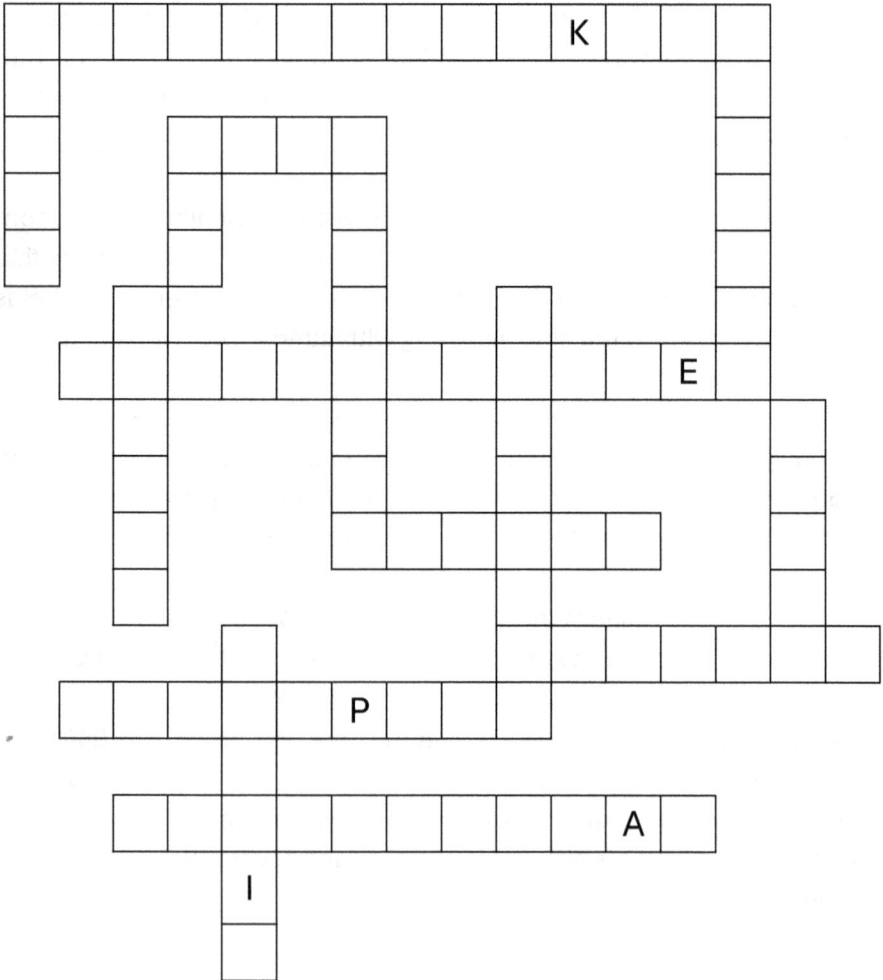

- 23 -

The name of a different part of the body is hidden in each of the sentences below. Can you find them all? The first has been filled in to get you started.

1. "How did you feel bowling for the match?"

    _____Elbow_____

2. "Today, we can't climb—rain is forecast!"

    _____

3. "I think the art is beautiful here."

    _____

4. "That's Tom, a childhood friend of Daniel..."

    _____

5. "...but Tom is taller than Daniel!"

    _____

6. "Look! Peter Pan creased my shirt!"

    _____

7. "In the wild, emus clean their nests every day."

    _____

8. "We often don't even do that!"

    _____

THE DOG THAT SURVIVED
A TSUNAMI

On March 11, 2011, a colossal magnitude 9.0 earthquake struck off the eastern coast of Japan. The epicenter was around 80 miles east of Sendai, a major industrial city and seaport on the Pacific coast of Japan's main island, Honshu. The quake was so sizable that it was felt as far away as eastern Russia, while the seabed beneath which it occurred was wrenched more than 30 ft upwards and thrown more than 150 ft sideways. This alone was enough to cause devastating damage to roads and buildings in and around Sendai—but the immense shifting of the sea floor off the Honshu coast then triggered a gigantic tsunami, which rolled outwards across the open ocean at speeds of up to 500 mph (eventually reaching as far away as Hawaii). The wave slowed as it grew in size and neared the Japanese coast, eventually reaching a height of up to 33 ft (10m) as it struck the land. Much of the coastal areas of Sendai—including the city's airport and nearby Fukushima nuclear reactor—were inundated with water, while in parts of the surrounding landscape the wave reached as far as 6 miles inland. In all, the disaster claimed the lives of more than 19,000 people and caused billions of dollars of damage.

In the aftermath of the earthquake, the Japanese government chartered dozens of planes and search vessels to scour the open ocean for any survivors who may have been swept out to sea. As the days and weeks went by, however, the likelihood of finding anyone alive became understandably slim—until, on April 2, three weeks after the original disaster, something truly remarkable happened.

Around one mile from the Sendai coast, out in the open water of the Pacific, one of the search vessels spotted a small brown dog standing atop the ruins of a house that had been swept out to sea. How long the dog at been at sea, and quite how it had managed to survive on its own for so long, was unknown, but as the dog was picked up and returned to the shore, news of its remarkable survival was soon making its way onto news channels the world over.

The dog had no identifying tags or chips, but as the story continued to make its way around the media, its owner recognized it immediately as her 2-year-old pup, Ban. A few frantic telephone calls to the authorities later, and Ban and his owner were reunited.

TOP 6 · FACTS
ANIMAL SURVIVAL & ESCAPEES

- In 1965, a golden eagle escaped from London Zoo and remained on the loose in the city for the next two weeks (becoming something of a local celebrity!). It was eventually recaptured and returned to the zoo, having been spotted enjoying the sites of the likes of Regent's Park, Euston Station, and Tottenham Court Road.

- In 1917, a stray puppy named Stubby (on account of his short tail) was adopted by a group of US infantrymen heading to the First World War. Stubby ended up accompanying his men to Europe, where he became adept at recognizing the smell of poisonous gas, responding to bugle calls, and even caught a German soldier who had sneaked into the trenches. After the war, Stubby was awarded a gold medal for his bravery.

- In December 2017, a tabby cat named Kylo followed his Scottish owner out into the street as he walked their family's dog, before disappearing into the Glasgow streets. His owners did not see Kylo again—until they received a phone call in September 2024, saying that he had been found and picked up by a local vet. Kylo was reunited with his owners that day, after going missing for seven years!

- In 1923, the Brazier family were visiting relatives in Indiana when their pet dog Bobbie was attacked by two strays and ran away. Despite an exhaustive search, Bobbie could not be found and the Braziers had to return home to Oregon without him. Three months later, however, Bobbie reappeared at the family home, having successfully navigated more than 2,500 miles of American wilderness.

- In 2014, an octopus was found trapped in a crayfish pot off the coast of Napier, New Zealand, and taken to the local aquarium. Nicknamed Inky, two years later the octopus managed to escape his tank, crawl unnoticed across the floor of the aquarium and down a drainage pipe that led directly back to the sea.

- In 2006, an otter named Jin escaped from her enclosure in Auckland Zoo, New Zealand, and swam 12 miles to Rangitoto Island, an isolated volcanic island in the Hauraki Gulf off the Auckland coast. She was found there a month later and returned to her enclosure.

- 24 -

The answer to each clue in this grid begins in the corresponding numbered square. The last letter of one answer is the first letter of the next.

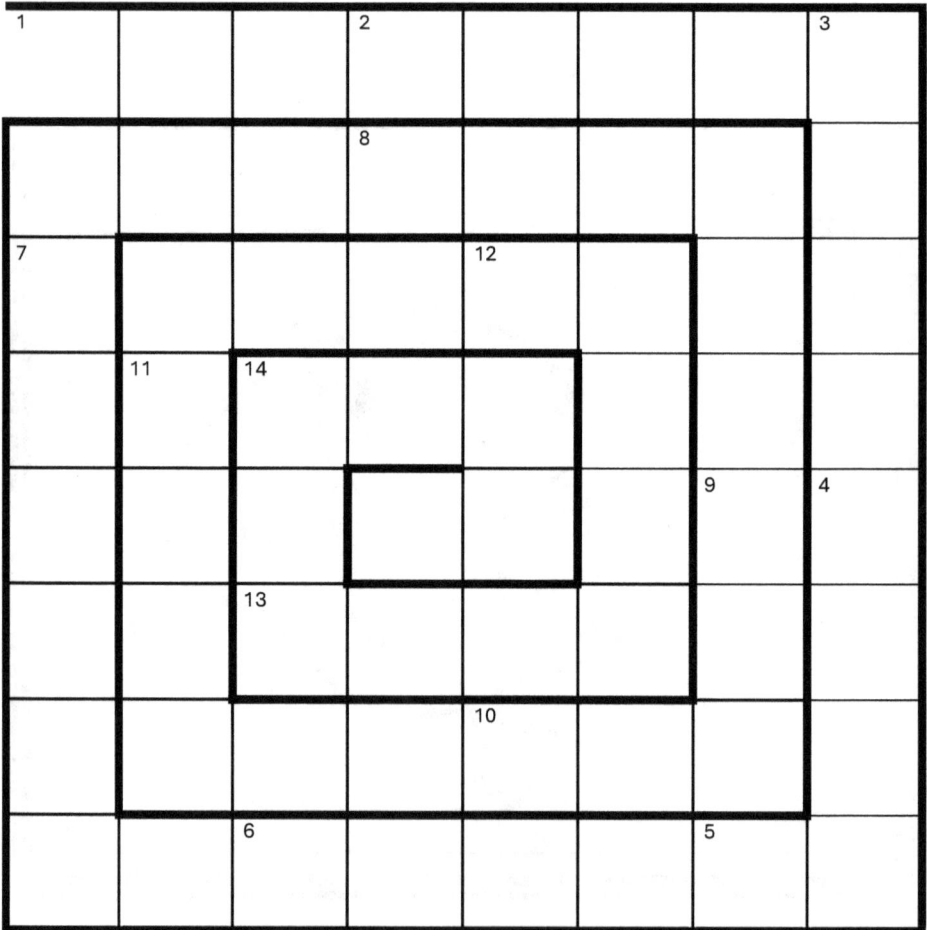

1. Leap

2. French capital

3. Not in use, left over

4. Consumed

5. Unpleasant

6. Young-looking

7. In or from the nearby area

8. Sweepstakes

9. Raising agent of bread

10. Working hard

11. Large, impressive

12. Catastrophe

13. Decay

14. Big cat

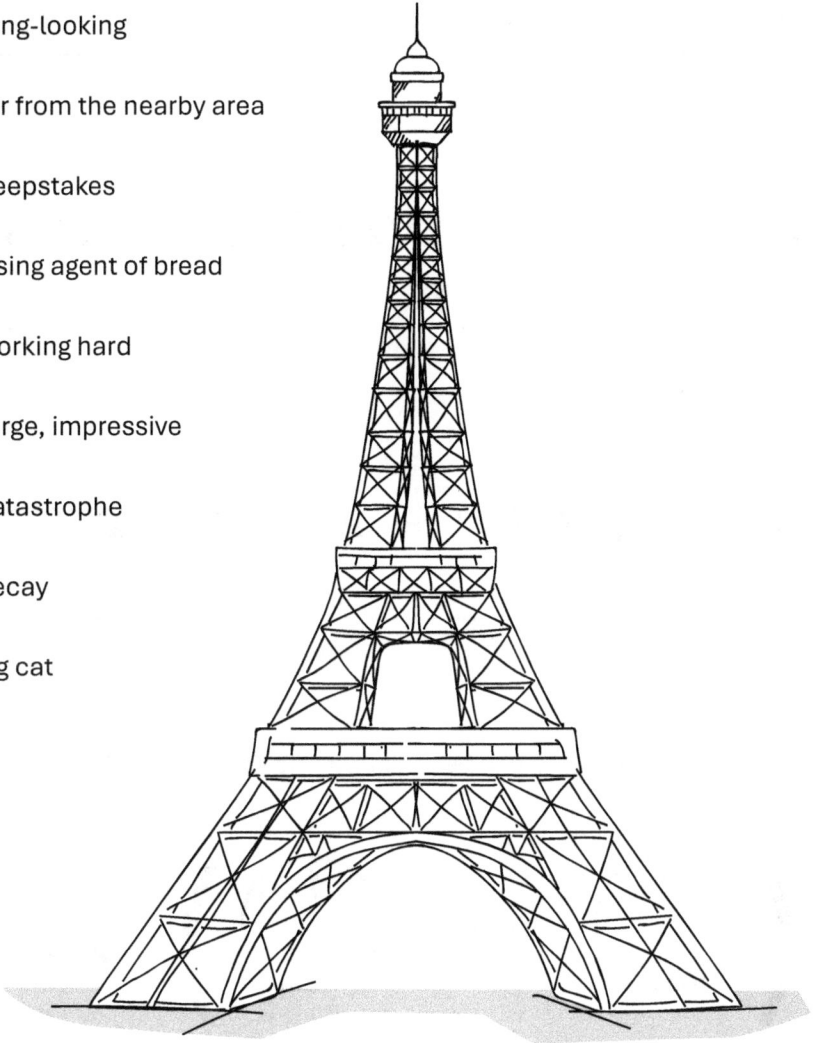

Each of the letters in the quotation below has been swapped for another.
Can you decode the message?

"X' DO EOOY ZVPAXYJ KXYUO X ZBK
YXYO.
" _' __ _EE_ _____I__ __N__ _
__S _____.

X' DO YODOP AYVZY B TXNO ZXSLYQS
_'V_ ____R ___W_ _ _ _____
___H____

B NXTG KOS!" – RBYXOT PBRUTXNNO
_ __L_ ___!" – _A____
__D___F__

What four-word phrase can be read from the figure below?

THE FIRST ACTOR TO PLAY
JAMES BOND IS ... NOT WHO YOU
THINK IT IS!

Ask any self-respecting movie buff who the first person to play James Bond was, and chances are they'll tell you it was Sean Connery in 1962's *Dr. No*. While it's certainly true that Connery was the first person to portray Bond on film, the question of who the first person to play James Bond at all, however, has a rather more surprising answer!

The character of James Bond was created by the English author Ian Fleming, who published the first of twelve novels featuring the character, *Casino Royale*, in 1953. The book was an immediate success, selling its entire first print within its first month on sale. Understandably, as the novel's popularity grew and the sales continued to increase, interest in adapting Fleming's novel for the big screen began to build. After several months of negotiations, in 1954 Fleming's publishers eventually signed a $1,000 deal (equivalent to more than $12,000 today) with American broadcasting network CBS, who wanted to adapt *Casino Royale* into a live one-hour television special, to be shown as part of their anthology drama series, *Climax*!

The story was adapted for the screen (with considerable edits, cutting it down to just 60 minutes) by Charles Bennett, an acclaimed serial writer whose previous credits had included several Alfred Hitchcock thrillers. Legendary character actor Peter Lorre was cast as the story's main villain, Le Chiffre, while the role of Bond was given to a relatively little known MGM performer and TV actor named Barry Nelson (perhaps best known for his performances in a handful of 1950s and 60s comedies and thrillers, including *Cactus Flower*, opposite Lauren Bacall). "At that time, no one had ever heard of James Bond," Nelson later commented. "I was scratching my head wondering how to play it [because] I hadn't read the book or anything like that." In fact, Nelson later admitted that he only took on the role because of the opportunity to act opposite Peter Lorre.

Ultimately, it was Nelson who became the first actor in history to portray the now-legendary James Bond, a full eight years before Sean Connery took on the role in *Dr. No*. But in those intervening years, someone else took a stab at the role too.

Robert Wentworth Holness was born in Vryheid in South Africa in 1928. Educated in England, he returned to South Africa in the 1950s, where he joined a theatre company in Durban. His work on the stage led to him taking a job at a local radio station in 1955, where he initially worked as an announcer and newsreader. In 1956, however, the station decided to broadcast an adaptation of Ian Fleming's latest James Bond novel, *Moonraker*—and cast Holness in the role as James Bond.

Holness later returned to the UK and continued to work in radio and television, eventually becoming the host of a long-running quiz show, *Blockbusters*, that proved successful enough to make him a household name—and has long overshadowed his place in James Bond lore as the second actor in history to take on the iconic role.

TOP 6 · FACTS
JAMES BOND

- Ian Fleming was just as suave and as well-traveled as the character he created. Born into a privileged family in England, he was educated in England, Germany, and Switzerland, worked as a journalist in Russia, served in naval intelligence during the war, and later moved to Jamaica, where he wrote most of his novels.

- The name of Fleming's estate in Jamaica, Goldeneye, was used as the title of the seventeenth James Bond movie in 1995.

- It has been suggested that James Bond's code number, 007, was taken from that of an Elizabethan spy, John Dee, who operated in the court of Elizabeth I. Long thought to be one of the queen's suitors, Dee would reportedly sign his private correspondence with her using the same number code later used by Bond.

- To date, the Bond movie franchise has earned almost $8 billion at the box office, making it the fifth most successful franchise in movie history.

- The James Bond books only truly became successful in the United States after President Kennedy named 1957's *From Russia with Love* as his favorite book in a newspaper interview. The 1963 movie adaptation (Sean Connery's second Bond film) was reportedly the last movie Kennedy watched before his death.

- When it came to thinking up a name for the suave, sophisticated, endlessly cool special agent he had created, author Ian Fleming wanted a short, punchy name. Picking up a copy of a bird book he kept in his study in Jamaica entitled *Birds of the West Indies*, he noted that it had been written by an ornithologist named James Bond, and the rest is history!

Can you match the cities on the left to the countries in which they are located? The first has been filled in for you to get you started.

Venice	Scotland
Shanghai	Mexico
Edinburgh	Italy
Istanbul	France
Guadalajara	Canada
Rio de Janeiro	China
Nice	Turkey
Vancouver	Brazil

Each of the 5-letter words below is missing its middle letter. Place those missing letters in the corresponding spaces in the grid, and a 7-letter word will be revealed reading down the central column. Watch out, though—there might be more than one possible missing letter for some words, but there is only one possible solution.

▼

N	O		E	L
T	H		N	K
S	I		C	E
S	T		P	S
V	E		A	N
S	H		L	L
F	O		C	E

What phrase has been encoded in the image below?

👁 4 👁, 🦷 4 🦷

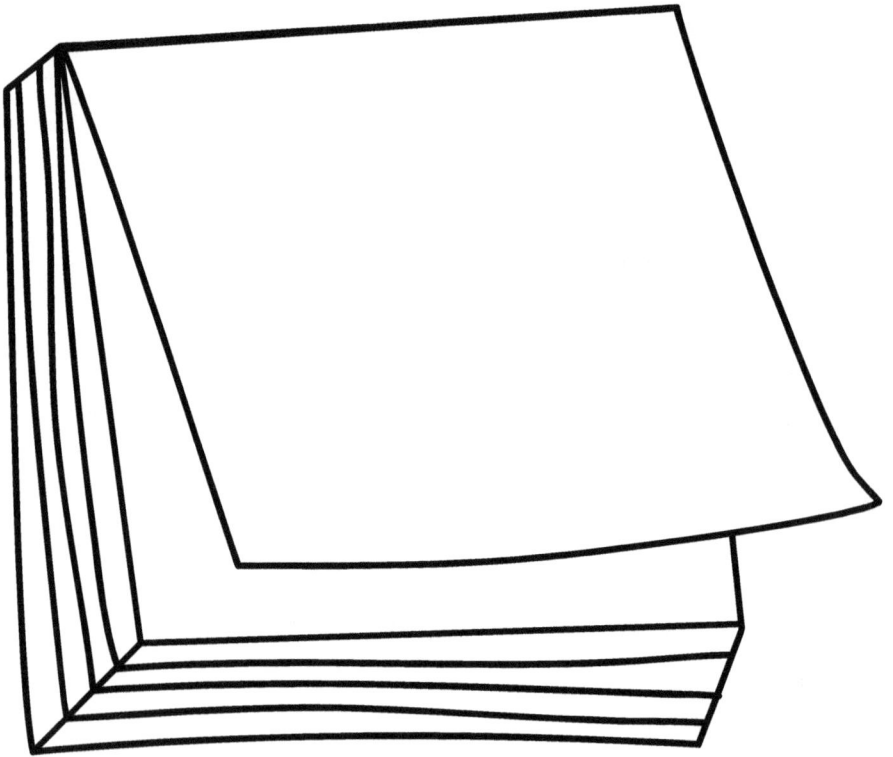

HOW THE POST-IT NOTE WAS INVENTED BY ACCIDENT

I t's one of the most useful and most widespread stationery products on the market. But the Post-It Note had a remarkably tricky beginning in the mid 1900s, which almost saw it never come to market at all.

The story begins in 1968, when an American research scientist named Spencer Silver was working in his laboratory at the famous 3M factory in St. Paul, Minnesota. Silver had been tasked with creating a specialist super-strong adhesive fluid that could be used by in the 3M factory's work in the aerospace industry. In fact, what he ended up somewhat accidentally creating was the complete opposite: a super-weak adhesive glue that could be used to stick something light to another surface, then removed with little effort at all, leaving no residue of the glue behind.

Because it was absolutely not what he was meant to have created, Silver thought of his creation as little more than a failure and took his research back to the drawing board. As for his super-weak adhesive? It was put into storage at the 3M labs and all but forgotten. Incredibly, Silver's glue was to remain in storage at the laboratory for the next six years, until a brainwave by one of his colleagues, Art Fry.

At church on the weekend, Fry had been struggling to keep his place among the pages in his hymn book. Remembering the super-weak adhesive Silver had created all those years ago, he took the sample back out of the 3M storage and began experimenting with adhesive bookmarks; as it happened, the only thing he had at his disposal that day were some loose scraps of yellow paper. Fry found that the glue was just tacky enough to allow him to keep his makeshift paper bookmarks in place, but not too tacky so as to damage the pages of his hymn book. The tests led to three years of further research and marketing, before finally, in 1977, the first Post-It Notes were put on sale at four cities across the Midwest, under the name Press 'N' Peel.

Bizarrely, fate had another stumbling block in the Post-It Note's history: the first Press 'N' Peel sales were disappointing, and with customers clueless as to what to do with them, 3M were forced to pull them from the shelves after just a few months on sale. Two further years of brainstorming and marketing were needed, before 3M took their product back to stores and offices across Boise, Idaho, in 1979. Free samples targeting office workers were mailed out, and this time the product was an instant hit; 90% of workplaces who received their free sample reordered the notes when they ran out!

The following year, the Post-It Note was put on sale nationally across the United States, and introduced to Canada and Europe in 1981. It quickly became an office stationery staple (no pun intended...), found on desks and in drawers all over the world. From a product that nearly didn't see the light of day at all, 3M now sells more than 50 billion individual Post-It Notes every year!

TOP 6 · FACTS
ACCIDENTAL INVENTIONS

- One of the most famous accidental discoveries was the antibiotic penicillin. In 1928, English scientist Alexander Fleming returned from vacation to find that one of the petri dish samples in his laboratory had become infested with mold; the area around the mold, however, was devoid of bacteria. Presuming that whatever the mold contained must have had antimicrobial properties, Fleming continued his research, leading to the world's first antibiotic medicine!

- In 1945, an engineer named Percy Spencer happened to walk past a magnetron—a kind of high-powered vacuum tube controlled by magnets—while holding a chocolate bar in his pocket. The chocolate melted in its wrapper, despite Spencer himself feeling no heat. The accidental discovery eventually led to the invention of the microwave!

- In 1943, a large coiled spring fell off the desk of a US engineer named Richard James. Noticing that the spring appeared to coil and uncoil itself as it "walked" down to the floor, James began working on a product that would do just that: he had invented the Slinky!

- In the 1930s, a Swiss inventor named Walter Jaeger began to experiment on an alarm-like detector that would be able to pick up on poisonous gases. Unfortunately (or so he thought) the detector he came up with kept detecting little more than the smoke from his cigarettes. Wisely seeing that this too might have useful properties, Jaeger's early experiments eventually led to the invention of the smoke detector.

- Way back in 1879, Russian chemical engineer Constantin Fahlburg had spent a day working with a mix of chemicals, chief amongst them coal tar. Having forgotten to wash his hands, Fahlburg happened to notice that everything he touched tasted sweet; the substance derived from coal tar that had coated his hands was later isolated as saccharine, the world's first artificial sweetener!

- Earlier still, in 1827 an English chemist named John Walker was mixing up a pot containing antimony sulfide and potassium chlorate (among other things) in his laboratory, when he noticed that a large clump of the material had stuck to the end of his stirrer. When he tried to scrape the material off, it burst into flames. He later refined the mixture—and ditched the stirrer!—and took his product to market as the world's first matchstick.

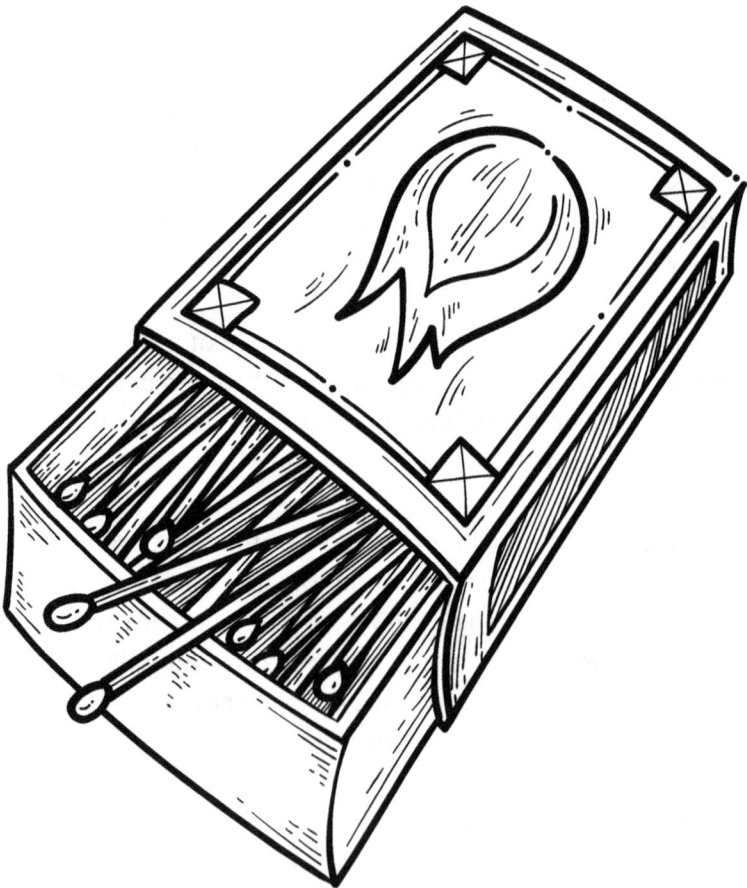

In each of the boxes below, the letters from two words that fit the corresponding subject category have been muddled up together. Can you unjumble them? The first has been filled in to get you started.

Bishop	**1. Chess pieces** **BEEHINOPQSU**	Queen
	2. Keyboard instruments **AAGINNOOPR**	
	3. Italian herbs **AABEGILNOORS**	
	4. They're seen in the sky **AABDEIILNPRR**	
	5. Prime numbers **EEEEFILNVV**	
	6. Caribbean islands **AAAABCCIJMU**	

Can you find your way through this maze from top to bottom?

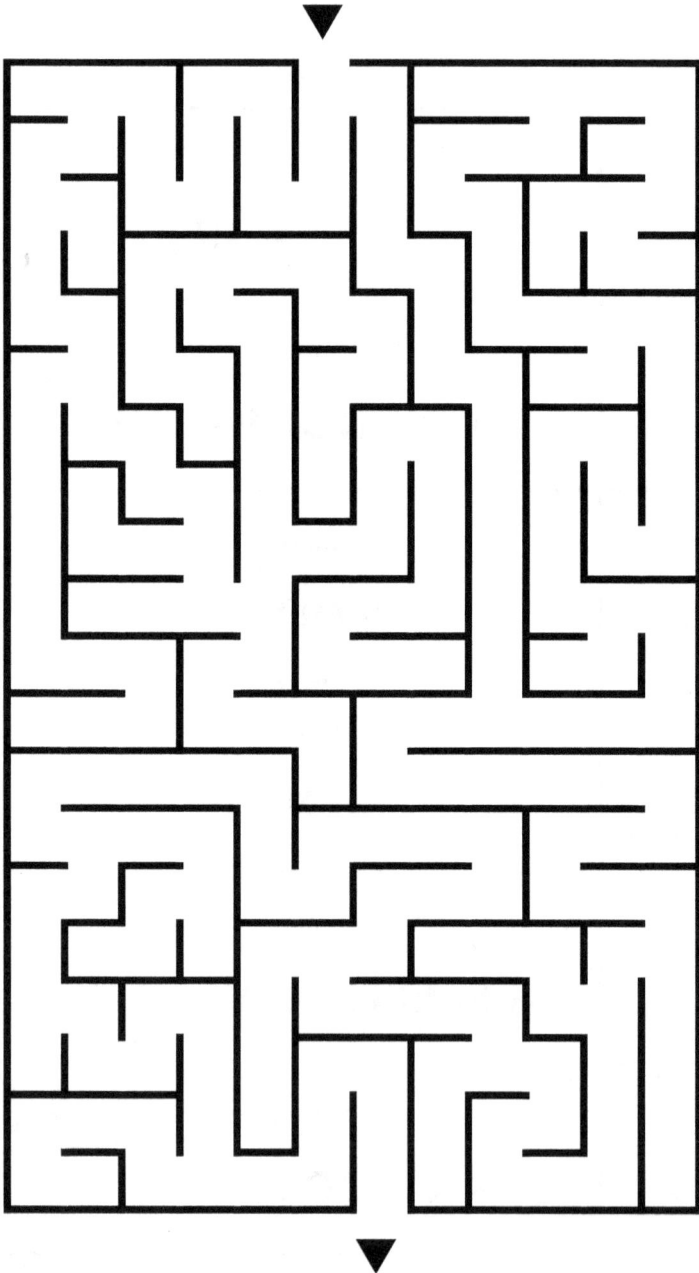

WHY 1729 IS KNOWN AS A TAXICAB NUMBER

Math is one of those subjects that you either love, or you hate (and that you're either good at, or terrible at!). But even the least mathematically minded of us know that certain numbers and groups of numbers have names.

Prime numbers, for instance, are all those that are only divisible by themselves and 1. Square numbers (indicated by a small raised 2) are the product of a number multiplied by itself—so 9 is the square of 3, as 3 multiplied by 3 makes 9. And cube numbers (indicated by a small raised 3) are the result of a number that is squared, and then squared again—so 27 is the cube of 3, because 3 multiplied by 3 makes 9, and 9 multiplied by 3 again makes 27. But what about taxicab numbers?

This particular numerical tale begins in London in the late 1910s. An English mathematician and both Cambridge and Oxford University scholar named GH Hardy had arrived in the city to visit his friend and former protégé, the Indian mathematician Srinivasa Ramanujan, who had taken ill with tuberculosis. Hardy hailed a cab and traveled across the city to get to Ramanujan's bedside at the sanatorium where he was receiving treatment.

The two began chatting in Ramanujan's room at the hospital, and in the conversation Hardy quipped that he hoped the fact that the number of the taxicab in which he had traveled across town—1729—was such a totally uninteresting one was not to be seen as a bad omen for his terribly unwell friend. To Hardy's surprise, however, Ramanujan explained that 1,729 was not "a rather dull" number, as Hardy had labeled it, but was in fact "very interesting number." As he explained, "It is the smallest number expressible as the sum of two cubes in two different ways."

What exactly does that mean? Well, as an arithmetic genius like Srinivasa Ramanujan would no doubt be able to point out, Ramanujan had noticed that 1,729 is equal to both 13 + 123, and 93 + 103. Or, to put it another way, $(1 \times 1 \times 1) + (12 \times 12 \times 12) = (9 \times 9 \times 9) + (10 \times 10 \times 10)$.

Sadly, Ramanujan's condition worsened shortly after his somewhat throwaway discovery, and after his death this anecdote—showing how even in his final days he was still a fountain of extraordinary knowledge about the world of numbers and mathematics—became a favored story of his friend, G.M. Hardy. As he continued to recount the tale to friends and colleagues, numbers that exhibit this kind of property came to be known as taxicab numbers in Hardy and Ramanujan's honor.

Amazingly (considering how quickly Ramanujan had been able to spot the peculiar significance of 1,729!), taxicab numbers like these are astonishingly rare, and in fact only six have so far been uncovered in over a century of further work. The smallest is technically 2 (which is the sum of 13 + 13, and vice versa), after which comes Ramanujan's 1,729. Then, there isn't another taxicab off the rank until 87,539,319—and after that, you'd have to wait until 6,963,472,309,248!

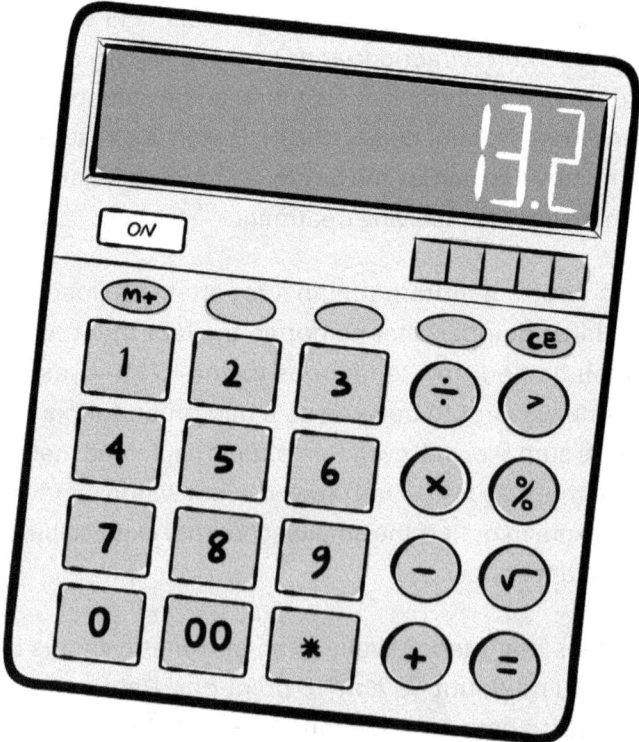

TOP 6 · FACTS
NUMBERS

- Every single number after the number 88 (eighty-eight) in English has an N in its name...

- ...but you don't need to use an A until you get to 1,000 (one thousand), unless you use the British names for the hundreds, such as 101 (one hundred and one)!

- $111{,}111{,}111 \times 111{,}111{,}111 = 12{,}345{,}678{,}987{,}654{,}321$

- 11 is one of the easiest numbers to multiply with. Single digits multiplied by 11 are simply repeated—so 2×11 is 22, $3 \times 11 = 33$, and so on—while to multiply two-digit numbers by 11, simply write their sum between them. So $17 \times 11 = 187$ (because $1 + 7 = 8$)!

- A number 1 followed by 100 zeroes is called a googol. 10 to the power of a googol is called a googolplex, while a shape with a googol of sides would be called a googolgon—though in practice, it would have so many sides that it would be all but indistinguishable from a perfect circle!

- The number 10 to the power of 10 to the power of 68, or $10^{10^{68}}$—that's a 1 followed by 100 million trillion trillion trillion trillion trillion zeroes!—has become known as a doppelgängion. In 2022, mathematician Antonio Padilla introduced the term as representative of the chances of bumping into someone exactly like you somewhere else in the universe!

The names of 14 American presidents are hidden in the grid below, but they're not in straight lines! Can you find all the names so that no letter is used more than once, and no letter is left over? The first answer has been filled in to get you started.

T	R	U	M	I	D	E	N	A	D
W	A	S	A	B	N	R	B	U	A
N	O	H	N	M	O	O	E	C	M
H	T	I	J	E	F	O	B	H	S
A	G	N	R	E	F	M	A	A	N
Y	E	S	S	O	N	C	M	A	A
R	O	O	N	V	A	K	L	E	N
V	E	S	O	B	N	I	C	V	D
E	L	T	S	U	R	N	Y	E	N
J	A	C	K	N	E	L	E	L	A

The eight numbers below have been removed from this magic square.

Place the numbers back in the grid so that the four boxes in each row and in each column total 42.

3 4 5 6 7 8 9 10

	13	16	
15			14
	18	11	
12			17

THE MAN WHO GAVE HIS NAME TO THE GUILLOTINE

You likely know that some inventions have been given the name of the person who invented them. Saxophones are named after a gentleman named Adolphus Sax. Pilates exercise routines were concocted by a man named Joseph Pilates. Graham crackers were named for the person who first made them too, the Reverend Sylvester Graham. And the very first modern Ferris wheel was designed and constructed by an engineer named George Washington Gale Ferris, Jr., as part of the 1893 World's Exposition in Chicago. In fact, from the Rubik's cube (named after Ernő Rubik) to the cowboy's Stetson hat (named after American hatmaker John B Stetson), you'll find so-called eponymous inventions like these in just about every industry—including, it seems, corporal punishment!

Of all the inventions to have taken the name of a real person, perhaps the guillotine is the most surprising. This brutal device—a razor-sharp blade, suspended above a stocks-like hole, through which the hapless victim would be made to place their head—was of course much used during the French Revolution in the late 1700s. And back then, it was given a name honoring that of a revolutionary leader and member of the French National Assembly, Joseph-Ignace Guillotin.

The guillotine itself might have Monsieur Guillotin's name, but it was not his work—and for that matter, despite his name now going down in history alongside one of the most bloodthirsty devices ever created, he wasn't all that keen on using it at all!

Guillotin was born in the picturesque town of Saintes, near Bordeaux in western France, in 1738. A doctor by trade, he graduated from university in Paris and alongside his medical work took a keen and rather prominent role in pre-Revolutionary politics. At that time in France, criminals and prisoners could be executed by any one of a number of increasingly bloody means, from hanging and decapitation with a sword (a punishment set aside for nobles and high-society types only), to dismemberment, burning, and even boiling (an especially brutal punishment used only for those found guilty of counterfeiting). By the end of the 1700s, however, French society was changing, and along with it, so too were opinions on the death penalty.

Guillotin himself was opposed to the death penalty and did not believe that the state should execute anybody, regardless of their crimes. The National Assembly, of which Guillotin was a member, did not quite agree with his abolitionist views, but they did nonetheless agree that a single method should be employed across the board, for all crimes and all people regardless of their social standing. Guillotin countered that whatever method that was to be, it should be as quick and as painless as possible—and with that in mind, he began championing the guillotine as the best option.

The guillotine itself, in fact, was invented by a surgeon named Antoine Louis (who tested his device's speed at lopping off heads by experimenting on dead bodies in a local Paris hospital!) For a time, it was yet another invention that came to share its inventor's name, and was known initially as the louisette. But after Dr. Guillotin began championing its use as the most humane way of executing criminals, it was his name that the device earned—and has kept ever since.

TOP 6 · FACTS
THINGS NAMED AFTER PEOPLE

- In 1907, a Belgian chemist named Leo Baekeland was experimenting with various chemicals in an attempt to invent a replacement for an expensive natural veneer named shellac. Instead, he invented a heat-resistant and durable polymer, which he named Bakelite—the world's first plastic!

- A staple of school science lessons the world over, the Bunsen burner is named after a German chemist named Robert Bunsen who invented it in 1855. Although the burner now bears his name, it is likely Bunsen's design was based on that of several earlier models, including one championed by the legendary scientist Michael Faraday!

- Perhaps one of the most surprising inventions named after its inventor is the sandwich, which takes its name from an 18th century English nobleman named John Montagu, the 4th Earl of Sandwich. According to legend, the Earl of Sandwich (a town in Kent, not far from London) used to request he be served meat and other foods placed between slices of bread while he played cards, so that the bread protected his fingers and stopped him getting the juices from the meat on his hand.

- Another English nobleman of the time was a British army officer named James Thomas Brudenell, the 7th Earl of Cardigan, in Wales. Brudenell was an acclaimed general who led the famous Charge of the Light Brigade during the Crimean War. He spent thousands of pounds of his own money kitting out his men in the best available kit, and in the 1830s, had his tailors create for them a special kind of buttoned tunic-like jacket—or as we know it today, a cardigan.

- The diesel engine and diesel fuel are both named after a German engineer named Rudolph Diesel (almost killing himself during the engine's development, when an early prototype exploded in his laboratory!).

- A movement favored by physical therapists and gym teachers everywhere, the burpee—in which a person lies down, gets to their feet, jumps in the air, and lies back down again—was developed as a test of fitness by a Columbia University student named Royal Burpee!

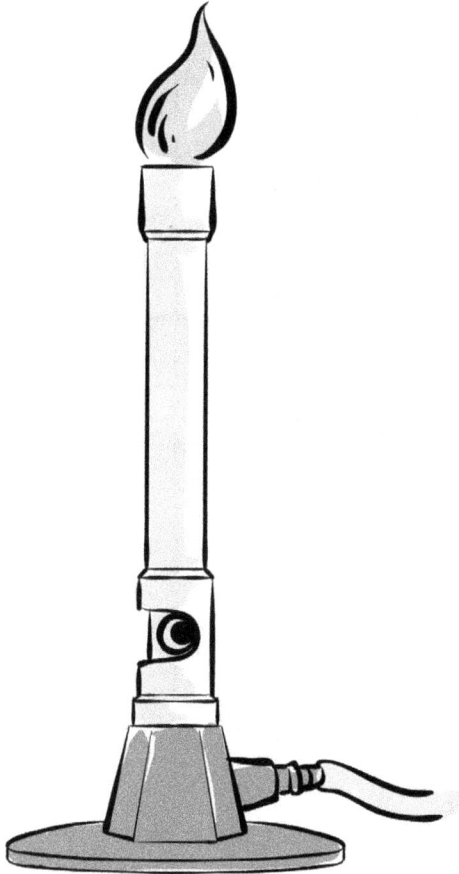

- 32 -

Fill in the grid below so that each row of nine squares, each column of nine squares, and each smaller 3 x 3 set of nine squares contain the digits 1–9 once and only once.

There can be no duplicate digits in any row, column, or smaller square.

Can you complete the grid correctly?

	4	8	6			9		1
			8	1			6	4
	6	1	4			7	2	8
4		2				3	8	9
			1	3			5	7
3	5				8	4	1	6
7		4	3		6	1	9	
	3							2
		6					4	

33

Complete the mini crossword below not by solving the clues, but by unjumbling them—each of the words in this puzzle are anagrams of their clue words.

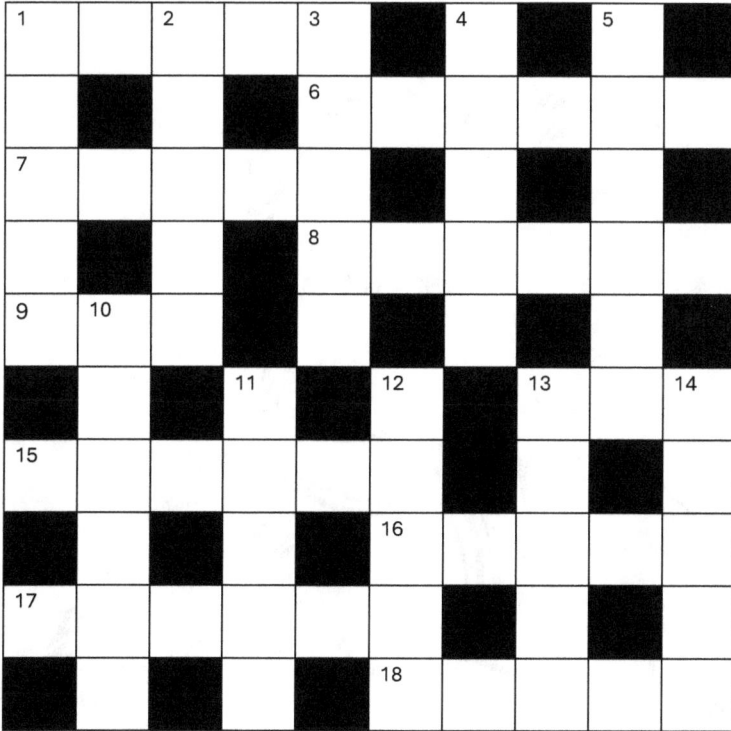

1		2		3		4		5	
				6					
7									
				8					
9	10								
			11		12		13		14
15									
					16				
17									
					18				

ACROSS

1. BEAMY
6. CATION
7. CODER
8. STATIN
9. CAT
13. SKA
15. MONDAY
16. MAINE
17. ITCHES
18. TENSE

DOWN

1. AIMED
2. CATHY
3. HEART
4. TASTE
5. PISTON
10. OOCYTE
11. STAIN
12. ASCOT
13. RAISE
14. PEEKS

PRESIDENT TAFT'S TOY POSSUMS

I f you're a history buff, you've perhaps heard the story of how the humble teddy bear came to be named after President Theodore "Teddy" Roosevelt.

This tale begins way back in November 1902, when Roosevelt was on a hunting trip to Mississippi. Unfortunately, while the rest of his hunting party had a successful day's shooting, the president looked to be coming home empty-handed when one of the group happened to come across a lone bear cub. Wanting to give the president the opportunity to shoot something that day, the man tied the cub up to a nearby willow tree, fetched President Roosevelt and the rest of the party, and began encouraging him to shoot the cub for sport.

Don't worry if you think that all sounds a little too brutal and bloodthirsty to ever be considered "sport", however—in fact, the president would agree with you! Not wanting to kill a defenseless creature, President Roosevelt had the cub released, and he returned to his accommodation empty-handed. This characteristic show of mercy, however, did not go down too well with everyone.

As word spread of Roosevelt's refusal to shoot the bear, the story eventually broke in the papers, and on November 16, 1902, a famous cartoon satirizing the event appeared in the *Washington Post*. A local store owner saw the cartoon and decided to seize on the popularity of the story by selling stuffed toy bears— which he labelled "Teddies"—in his shop. The toys proved hugely popular, and we've be snuggling up to teddy bears ever since.

After Roosevelt left office, however, toy makers were keen to continue the vogue for soft toys with something new. And with a new president, William Howard Taft, now installed in the White House, they were keen to ensure that whatever new toy they worked on had a similarly presidential backstory—and looked to Taft for inspiration.

By now, it was January 1909, and Taft was the president-elect awaiting his inauguration. In his honor, a banquet was arranged in Atlanta, at which the president-in-waiting requested he and his guests be served platters of "possum and taters"—that is, sweet potatoes served alongside a whole baked opossum. And at the end of the meal, the president was presented with a toy stuffed possum, named "Billy," which he was assured was to be just as big a hit as his predecessor's teddy bears. Alas, the toy makers who believed that to be true were completely wrong.

Proving that fads and trends can never be intentionally manufactured, despite "Billy Possum" toys, pins, and other paraphernalia flooding the market in 1909, they had all but disappeared by the end of the year, as the teddy bear craze refused to die down. President Roosevelt may have left office, but his lasting impression on the toy market had not gone with him!

TOP 6 · FACTS
TOYS AND GAMES

- Such is the complexity of the rules and the sheer number of playing pieces and potential moves in a game of chess that it has been suggested we might never know for sure how many games of chess are mathematically possible. In fact, there are more possible chess games than there are atoms in the universe!

- The character that you operate on in a game of Operation is called Cavity Sam.

- It has been estimated that more than 1 billion people around the world have played a game of Monopoly.

- When you pick your first seven tiles out of the bag at the start of a game of Scrabble, you have around a 15% chance of picking a set of letters from which you can immediately make a 7-letter word. (Whether you know enough 7-letter words to know what word you can spell, however, depends on how good a Scrabble player you are!)

- In 2015, the official French-language Scrabble championship was won by a New Zealander named Nigel Richards—who didn't speak French!

- The oldest playable board game in the world is called The Royal Game of Ur. Played in the ancient Mesopotamian city of Ur, in modern-day Iraq, boards and counters for playing the game have been found to date back to at least 4,600 years!

Grab the shampoo—the theme of this wordsearch is hair and haircare!

BLOWDRY   **COMB**   **CONDITIONER**   **CURLER**
CURLING IRON   **FOLLICLE**   **GEL**   **HAIRDRYER**
HAIRSPRAY   **PERM**   **SCALP**   **SHAMPOO**
STRAIGHTENERS   **STYLE**   **WAX**

```
N Z C U R L I N G I R O N W F I K
D O O P M A H S D O Z V A Q M N H
F H A I R S P R A Y R X P W B Q X
T O C E X Y C R O F E E J I M W Z
S X R O P Z R R P Y Y U I B L A I
T B T I N F X C W T R S K P Q Y R
R C Z R D D C M E V D Y A U P O P
A H H F W X I M B Z R I B E M A E
I S C A L P Z T D C I L N J D S R
G M J C D U X E I R A H E U F C M
H C R B A R A B S O H L Y Q A L B
T H Z K M H E I R D N E X B M O C
E J J Q A C J L S H K E W J D V J
N K O A W L E G R T M R R V G F E
E E L C I L L O F U Y W B K E S O
R F X O E S H D U E C L O J M S I
S R X D B L O W D R Y N E B E P W
```

Place the six three-by-three grids of letters below into the grid at the bottom of the page so that six 9-letter words can be read across each of the rows.

L	P	H
R	T	S
H	E	S

I	A	L
A	R	E
I	F	F

C	E	L
C	O	U
O	R	C

E	D	I
C	H	I
P	L	A

O	N	E
H	I	P
T	R	A

T	O	R
L	D	C
I	N	T

AUSTRALIA'S EMU WAR

Birds like ostriches and emus might not be able to fly, but they still have wings. It is their sheer size that renders their wings all but useless for flight, as a typical ostrich might stand anywhere from 6 to 9 ft tall and weigh upwards of 280 lb, while an emu is slightly smaller, standing around 5ft tall and coming in a little over 100 lb.

What birds like these lack in their ability to fly, however, they make up for in their ability to run. Despite their large size, ostriches and emus can reach running speeds of around 30–40 miles per hour, while a sprinting ostrich can cover as much as 16 ft in a single stride. And back in November 1932, the Australian military found out just how flighty and powerful large birds can be when they somewhat bizarrely went to war against the country's emus.

Following the First World War, the government of Western Australia began offering incentives to returning soldiers to venture out into the western Outback and begin developing the land for farming, providing food and crops for the country's growing population. More than 5,000 men accepted the government's invitation, and farms and fields began springing up all across Western Australia. Unfortunately, the government's scheme was somewhat shortsighted. The soil in the Outback is notoriously poor, while the scorching hot climate away from Australia's coast makes growing and farming delicate food crops all but impossible. Not only that, but the farmers' fields began popping up across migration routes that had long been used by Australia's emus; as the seasons changed, thousands of the gigantic birds began moving across the farms, pulling down fences, drinking watering holes dry, and gobbling up what little crops the farmers had been able to grow. After an especially tough drought hit Australia's western region in the early 1930s, the yearly arrival of the migrating emus in its wake proved the last straw, and the farmers demanded the government take action. Their response what somewhat unexpected: they went to war.

Trucks full of troops armed with machine guns were sent out into the Western Australian Outback, tasked with mowing down as many of the birds as they could. The entire scheme, however, quickly descended into complete and utter chaos when it was revealed that after three days of "fighting," the soldiers had only managed to kill 30 birds.

Incredibly, rather than rethink the operation, the government and military doubled down, sending yet more men and more weapons—and considerable cost to the public finances—to tackle the situation. The extra manpower and ammunition understandably helped, but after almost two months, the soldiers had still only managed to kill around 2,500 emus—a tiny fraction of the country's population.

Even these numbers have long been disputed, and it is likely the number of birds actually killed in the so-called Emu War of 1932 was not even as high as that. Finally, it was realized that the sheer cost of the project and number of bullets required to bring down a single bird was too great for the cull to continue, and the entire scheme came to an embarrassing end early in 1933.

TOP 6 · FACTS
FLIGHTLESS BIRDS

- Worldwide, there are around 60 species of flightless birds, including ostriches, emus, cassowaries, and penguins. It is thought more than 150 flightless species have gone extinct.

- The kiwi is one of the world's strangest flightless birds. Native only to New Zealand, is feathers are so narrow as to be more like fur than plumage, and it is the only bird in the world whose nostrils are at the end of its beak.

- The world's smallest flightless bird is the so-called Inaccessible Island rail, a 6-inch water bird that lives only on a tiny isolated island (hence its name!) in the Southern Atlantic Ocean. The island is so remote that scientists have long wondered how the birds arrived there despite their inability to fly, but it is now thought the birds descended from a flighted species of water rail that flew to the island to breed, and there gradually lost their ability to fly.

- The kakapo is the only species of flightless parrot in the world. Native to New Zealand, the bird is mainly nocturnal and jogs along the ground searching for food among the leaf litter.

- Antarctica is so white and so sparse that the colonies of emperor penguins that nest there can be seen clearly and counted from space!

- The takahe is another kind of water rail and flightless bird native to New Zealand. It was long thought to have gone extinct when a population of the birds was unexpectedly discovered in an isolated valley in New Zealand more than 50 years after the last bird was seen in the wild.

The 15 H words and phrases listed below connect together in the grid. Can you find the right place for each one?

HAIR'S-BREADTH **HARSH** **HASH** **HAWFINCH**
HEATH **HELLISH** **HEMSWORTH** **HETEROTROPH**
HI-TECH **HOGWASH** **HOOCH** **HOPSCOTCH**
HUH **HURRAH** **HUSH**

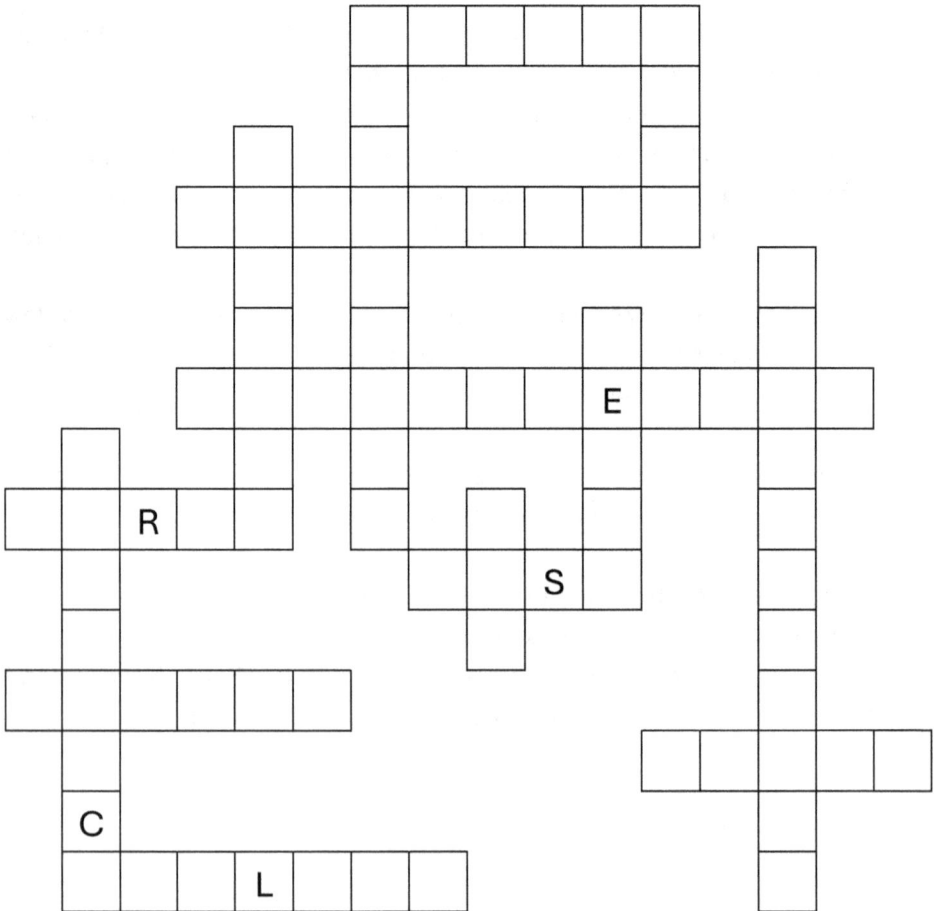

- 37 -

The 16 words and phrases in the grid below can be arranged into four connected groups of four—that is, with each set of four answers having something in common.

Can you work out the connections? Be careful, though—some answers might belong in more than one group, but there is only one overall solution!

Lock	Hound	Old movie	Unicorn
Mermaid	Cyclops	Piano	Panda
Zebra	Car	Lion	Door
Dalmatian	Fairy	Beast	Phoenix

HOW THE BRITISH ROYAL FAMILY CHANGED THE LENGTH OF THE OLYMPIC MARATHON

The Olympic marathon running race famously takes its name from the town of Marathon, in Attica, Ancient Greece, which was the site of a battle in 490 BC. Greece had been invaded by the Persians, and an army of local Athenian soldiers was sent out to the battlefield to repel them. Incredibly, the Athenians defeated the Persians—the first Persian invasion of mainland Greece—in a single afternoon, and in the aftermath of the battle, a soldier named Pheidippides was given the task of running from Marathon to Athens to bring news of their victory to the city. The distance Pheidippides ran is thought to have been around 25 miles, and it was this length that formed the basis of the modern marathon race when a plan was hatched to recreate Pheidippides' extraordinary feat as an athletic feat at the first modern Olympic Games back in 1896.

Today, a modern marathon race is now standardized not at 25 miles, but precisely 26 miles and 385 yards—or exactly, 42,195 meters. But this length has only been the standard length of a marathon since 1924; in the first few decades of the modern Olympic Games, the marathon race varied slightly in length, between around 24 and 26 miles, depending on the route, course, and city in which the Games were held.

At those very first modern Olympics, held in Athens in 1896, for instance, athletes retraced the course ran by Pheidippides—from Marathon to the Greek capital—and as such completed a roughly 25-mile race; appropriately enough, it was won by a local Greek athlete named Spyridon Louis. At the 1900 Games in Paris, however, the course was a little over 25 miles; four years later in St. Louis, it was slightly shorter, at 24 miles and 1,500 yards; and then in London in 1908, it was set at 26 miles and 385 yards—the length of the race today. And oddly, the reason for this curiously precise distance has less to do with Pheidippides' race, and more to with Britain's royal family!

When it was decided that there would be a marathon race at the 1908 London Olympics, a plan was put in place to have the race begin at Windsor Castle and finish in front of the royal box at London's famous White City Stadium, so that it could be spectated at both ends by members of the royal family. Having run 26 miles from Windsor, it was arranged that runners would then enter the stadium and complete an almost entire clockwise lap—but not quite a full 400 meter lap—of the surrounding athletic track. That thereby ensured the runners finished, not where they entered the stadium, but directly in front of the watching royals. As a result, the race was run over a distance of 26 miles, plus 385 yards.

In the decades that followed the 1908 London Games, the distance of the Olympic marathon continued to fluctuate, as different cities followed suit and adopted their own routes and tracks. At the 1924 Games, again in Paris, however, it was decided that the distance should be standardized, thereby allowing records to stand and be compared from one marathon to the next.

TOP 6 · FACTS
THE OLYMPIC GAMES

- A marathon race has been included in the Olympic Games every year since they were revived in 1896, but all the initial competitors were male. In fact, the length of the race—and the level of endurance involved—was deemed so great that a female Olympic marathon was not held until 1984!

- The early Olympic Games included several sports no longer contested at the Games today. Among the very first Olympic events were bizarre pursuits such as rope climbing, tug-of-war, and even firefighting!

- The medal given out at the 1900 Olympic Games in Paris were rectangular. This is the only time in the modern Olympics' history that the winners' medals have not been round.

- It's not just the medals that were different in the early years of the Olympics, too: in some of the early competitions, winning athletes were given prizes such as silverware, trophies, works of art, and even clocks!

- Originally too, first-place athletes were awarded silver, not gold; bronze was given to the runner-up; and there was no prize at all for third place.

- One of the greatest early Olympians was an Australian rower named Henry Pearce. During the 1928 Games in Amsterdam, he stopped his boat to allow a family of ducks to safely swim across his lane, yet still won the race!

- 38 -

The answer to each clue in this grid begins in the corresponding numbered square. The last letter of one answer is the first letter of the next.

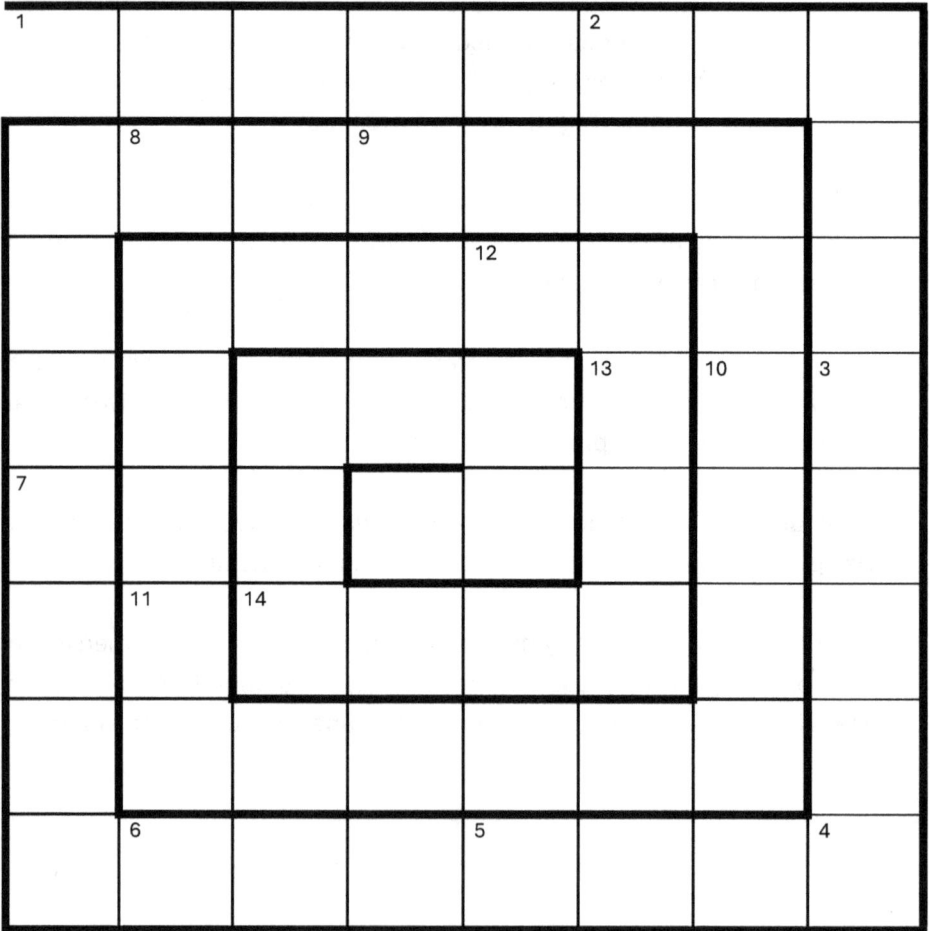

1. Contusion, mark on the skin from a bump

2. Large birds of prey

3. Traditionally lucky number

4. Pleasant

5. Make money

6. Hangman's knot

7. Ahead of time

8. Word of agreement

9. Dish for holding a cup

10. Diner, eatery

11. Very smallest

12. Number in a duo

13. Sprint faster than

14. Digits, figures

39

Each of the letters in the quotation below has been swapped for another. Can you decode the message?

" 'VGQFP' FB OAX F GV XW LAC
" '___I_' __ _H_ _ _M_N __E

RGBYCLRGSS PXMNL. CGNUFW FB
_____TB___ C__R_. ___V__ _S

OAX F GV." – VGQFP HXAWBXW
___ _ A_." – __G__ _____O_

What three-word phrase can be read from the figure below?

ALL
ALL
ALL
ALL

THE LOVE TRIANGLE GRAFFITI OF POMPEII

G iven that the entire site is now little more than a museum, it's easy to forget that the ruins of the Roman city of Pompeii—destroyed by the eruption of the volcano Mount Vesuvius in AD 79—was once a bustling and thriving city, just like the nearby towns and cities that surround it today. And just like a modern town, Pompeii had its fair share of local stories and intrigues—some of which we are still privy to today thanks to a rather unexpected archeological artifact.

Scattered among the surviving walls and buildings of the town are some prime examples of Ancient Roman graffiti. Just like people today, the citizens of Pompeii—and most other Roman towns and cities across the Empire—would often daub their thoughts and opinions onto walls for all the locals to see. In fact, graffiti was so common in towns like Pompeii that it seems the Romans viewed the walls of their buildings as little more than a public message board on which to record the day's events, reconnect with friends, or even air grievances. "All the finances officer of the Emperor Nero," wrote one person in Pompeii who was apparently none too happy with a meal he had been served locally, "says this food is poison!" Another would-be critic who was, it seems, not too happy with the quality of the wine at a local bar in Pompeii wrote, "Would that you pay for all your tricks, innkeeper! You sell us water and keep the good wine for yourself" on the wall of a workshop next door.

This being the Romans, of course, a great deal of the graffiti that has been unearthed is more than a little vulgar, with many of the locals making jokes and comments about their (and their neighbors') toilet habits. Others, however, were just happy to leave their mark. "Aufidius was here. Goodbye!" wrote a gentleman (presumably named Aufidius!). "Antiochus hung out here with his girlfriend Cithera," has been found written on the walls of the gladiators' barracks. And on the wall of a bar, two good friends commemorated a (presumably very good) night out with the words, "We two dear men, friends forever, were here. If you want to know our names, they are Gaius and Aulus."

One of the most scandalous examples of Pompeii's graffiti, however, is a back-and-forth scrawled onto the wall of a local caupona (a kind of Ancient Roman saloon), between two local men both attempting to attract the attention of the barmaid. "Successus the Weaver loves a barmaid named Iris, who does not care about him," reads the first line, "and the more he begs, the less she cares." Below that admission, however, is a note from an apparent rival for Iris' love, reading, "You who are bursting with jealousy, do not dare to bother someone who is more attractive than you." And then below that, finally, is the payoff. "I've said it, I've written it. You love Iris, who does not care about you."

This final line is signed "Severus," suggesting that it was Severus who began the argument, revealing Successus' love for Iris, before the two began their back-and-forth. Precisely what the result of their argument was (and what Iris thought of them, for that matter), is sadly a secret now lost to the town and its destruction!

TOP 6 · FACTS
POMPEII

- There were signs that Pompeii was not in a particularly safe location long before it was built: the town stood on a vast lava plateau, around 130ft above sea level, created by countless earlier volcanic eruptions. On top of the plateau, moreover, lay at least three thick layers of fertile black sediment, likely deposited by landslides.

- Some of the town's residents were extraordinarily well-to-do, with lavish villas and grand open gardens unearthed among the rubble. One house even had a stable of thoroughbred horses, all wearing bronze trappings.

- On the day of the eruption of Vesuvius, some of the residents of Pompeii suffered terrible deaths. One man was even decapitated in the disaster, either from a large rock thrown from the volcano, or by something in his home that was blown loose by the eruption and fired at him like a projectile!

- The entire town of Pompeii was so decimated by the eruption that it was lost until the mid 1700s.

- Pliny the Elder, a Roman naturalist and officer who aided in the evacuation of the area after the eruption, was one of several important names who died in the eruption. He was last seen on a beach, having guided a group away from the town in an ill-fated attempt to escape the eruption by sea. Two days after the eruption, his body was found on the same beach, having apparently succumbed to the toxic gases from the volcano.

- Much of what we know about Pliny's death—and about the events of the day Pompeii was destroyed—comes from his nephew, Pliny the Younger, who was just 17 at the time and living in relative safety further along the Bay of Naples. He recorded the details of the day in a letter to a local historian, named Tacitus.

Listed on the left here are the names of various foods and drinks. On the right are the kind of foods that each one is. Can you match them up?
The first has been completed to get you started.

Earl Grey	Apple
Ciabatta	Wine
Pinto	Bean
Pistachio	Bread
Cappuccino	Soup
Golden Delicious	Nut
Beaujolais	Tea
Minestrone	Coffee

In the grid below, draw lines connecting A to A, B to B, C to C, D to D, and E to E.

You may only use horizontal or vertical lines, so no diagonal lines are allowed. No line must cross another connecting line.

The connecting lines you draw must pass through all the empty squares, leaving none empty once all the letters are connected. However, no empty square can be used more than once.

A							
		D			D	E	
		B	A		C		
C					E	B	

THE ALLIGATORS THAT LIVED AT THE WHITE HOUSE

The White House—at 1600 Pennsylvania Avenue, Washington, DC—has been the official residence of every American president since John Adams, during whose presidency the capital of the United States was relocated to Washington from Philadelphia.

In those intervening two centuries or so, the House has seen its fair share of history, including the memorable day in 1814, when British troops attempted to set it on fire. (Contrary to popular history, however, that is not why the House was painted white; far from covering up the scorch marks of an attempted British conflagration, the House was first painted white when it was completed in 1798, as a coating of lime-based whitewash was added to help keep the underlying stonework waterproof!) But the White House has also seen quite a few passing residents, understandably—and perhaps none are more unusual than a pair of alligators that reportedly called the White House home in the 1820s, during the presidency of John Quincy Adams.

According to White House legend, shortly after he was inaugurated as America's sixth president, John Quincy Adams was gifted a pet alligator (or, according to other versions of this tale, several baby alligators) by Gilbert du Motier, the Marquis de Lafayette.

A French nobleman who had earlier volunteered in the Continental Army and served under George Washington, de Lafayette returned to France towards the turn of the 19th century, where he helped to draw up the French Declaration of Rights and assisted in the Storming of the Bastille. Forced into exile and having refused to serve under Napoleon Bonaparte, de Lafayette was invited back to America in 1824 by Adams' predecessor, President James Monroe. He gladly accepted and arrived back in the United States to a hero's welcome before embarking upon a lengthy tour of all 24 of the states of the Union at that time. De Lafayette's tour lasted so long that he ended up spending the bitter winter of 1824–25 at the White House. As a result, he was there when John Quincy Adams came to power in the 1824 election, before setting off to complete his tour of the southern states early the following year. Quite what happened next is unclear, but if legend is to be believed, de Lafayette returned to Washington from America's southernmost regions armed with at least one alligator, which he gifted to President Adams at the White House before returning to France. And what did the president do with this pet alligator? Well, with few other options, he simply kept the reptile in the unfinished East Room bathroom (and would reportedly delight in sending unwanted house guests there to use the facilities, only for them to flee the room in terror!).

Unfortunately, despite records of the presidential alligators dating back to the 1800s, White House historians have never been able to full verify this tale, leading some to believe that it is nothing more than legend. On the other hand, however, there are those who believe no such story would surely ever have come about without at least some kernel of truth—so who knows, perhaps there really was an alligator in the White House bathroom after all!

TOP 6 · FACTS
PRESIDENTIAL PETS

- During the Second World War, President Roosevelt was so often seen with his beloved pet dog Fala that his security detail gave the dog its own nickname—"The Informer."

- The first president born west of the Appalachians (in a log cabin, no less) Andrew Jackson was known for his tough temperament and no-holes-barred attitude—something which he apparently passed on to his pet parrot, which had a reputation for its fondness for swearing. Unfortunately, the parrot eventually outlived the president and caused such a ruckus at Jackson's funeral that it had to be removed from the ceremony!

- During the First World War, Woodrow Wilson and his family aided in the war effort by allowing a flock of four dozen sheep to graze on the White House lawn. President Taft also kept a cow on the White House lawn named Pauline Wayne.

- Among some of the other strangest-named presidential pets were George Washington's hound Sweetlips, Herbert Hoover's pet dog King Tut, and Calvin Coolidge's collie, Prudence Prim.

- Lyndon Johnson kept two pet beagles at the White House, with arguably the least inspired names of all: they were called Him and Her!

- Theodore Roosevelt returned to the White House from a trip west in 1903 with a live badger that he gifted to his son, Archibald.

In each of the boxes below, the letters from two words that fit the corresponding subject category have been muddled up together. Can you unjumble them? The first has been filled in to get you started.

Arial	**1. Common typefaces** **AAACCIILMNORSS**	*Comic Sans*
	2. Middle East nations **AAAIQRRSTY**	
	3. 2020s Super Bowl champions **ACEEEFGHILSS**	
	4. Ingredients in a salad **ACEELMOOTTTTU**	
	5. Household things put on the floor **ADGMOORRTU**	
	6. Lizards **AAACEEGHILMNNOU**	

- 43 -

The name of a musical instrument is hidden inside each of the sentences below. Can you find them all? The first has been filled in to get you started.

1   "I thought it might tip <u>Ian o</u>ver the edge!"

       <u>   Piano   </u>

2   "Do you want whiskey not rum, Peter?"

       _____

3   "Wendy is Austrian, Glenda is Swiss."

       _____

4   "Unfortunately, he's had the flu ten days in a row!"

       _____

5   "We're going to have to cancel Lola's party."

       _____

6   "What did the woman do, Linda?"

       _____

7   "A barrel, a tub, a cask, and a keg."

       _____

8   "Who's the best, Dumbledore or Gandalf?"

       _____

THE GLADIATORS WHO WERE SO WELL MATCHED THEY DECLARED A DRAW

The Colosseum in the center of Rome is no doubt one of the most famous Roman buildings in all of Europe. Properly known as The Flavian Amphitheater, the Colosseum was completed under the so-called Flavian emperors of Rome—a thirty-year dynasty of Roman rulers who succeeded the emperor Nero—in the 1st century AD. Over the centuries that followed, the remarkable structure played host to all manner of battles and spectacles of increasing size and scale. Wild animals (including lions and tigers), chariot races, public executions, and even staged sea battles were all held within its walls, all as entertainment for hundreds of Roman spectators, including the emperor and his companions. But of all the Colosseum's battles, one of the most remarkable is also one of its subtlest: a one-on-one fight between two of Rome's most admired and most talented gladiators.

This story took place in 80 AD, shortly after the Colosseum was completed under the Flavian emperor Titus. As part of the inaugural games and entertainment put on to showcase the building to the people of the city, it was arranged for two of the most popular gladiators of the day—Priscus and Verus—to fight one another, man to man. Their fight was to be the highlight of the Colosseum's opening day of events, a true spectacle of skill and bloodthirstiness in front of the baying crowd. But as their battle began, it soon became clear that the pair were precisely equally matched.

All that we know of Priscus and Verus' fight comes from a poem written by the Roman writer Martial to celebrate the opening day of the Colosseum. As he records, the two men began fighting, and continued fighting, and still continued fighting—with no man securing victory, nor resigning from the fight. And the longer they fought, the more it became clear that there would be no victor here at all; the duo were as strong and as skilled as one another and could conceivably continue fighting one another for many hours to come.

With no obvious victor on the cards, Martial writes that the emperor, Titus, decided to step in and declared Priscus and Verus' battle to be a draw. At long last, Martial recorded, "an end was however found for the well-matched contest: equal they fought, equal they resigned." Rather than have one gladiator take home the victor's prize, "Caesar [the emperor] sent wands to each man ... such was the reward that their valor received."

Unlike what we're often shown in the movies, it is certainly true that not all gladiatorial battles ended with the death of one of the combatants; occasionally, if one fighter found himself totally outclassed by his opponent, he could raise his hands in surrender and end the fight prematurely. (This was understandably not popular with the crowds but gave the fighter the opportunity to return to his training and give the audience a better show next time.) The announcement of a draw, however, was uncommon: as Martial wrote, "Under no other prince save thee, Caesar, has this ever happened—that, when two fought with each other, both were victors."

TOP 6 · FACTS
GLADIATORS

- Not all gladiatorial fighters fought in the same way, nor wielded the same weapons. A fighter called a *retiarius*, for instance, was armed with a trident, rather than a sword, and carried a weighted net with which to entangle his opponent.

- Not all the gladiators were slaves or prisoners forced to fight, either. As the popularity of gladiatorial combat grew in Ancient Rome, scores of private citizens signed up to become gladiators, lured by the thrill of the celebrity and respect that came with it.

- Some emperors gamely joined in the events of the Colosseum (albeit using specially dulled weapons and from a position of obvious safety!). Among the many rulers to have stepped onto the Colosseum's floor to fight over the years are Titus himself, Caligula, and Commodus—who is recorded as throwing a spear at a panther!

- In the movies, the emperor giving the "thumbs down" gesture is often seen as a sentence of death in the Colosseum, but this is just for our modern eyes. In fact, some historians believe a "thumbs up" gesture was more likely a sign that the gladiator was to be killed.

- Specialist fighters named *venatores*, or *bestiarii*, were trained in the art of hunting and fighting animals, not other gladiators. As well as lions and other big cats, among the many animals the Colosseum played host to over the centuries were ostriches, crocodiles, elephants, and even bears!

- Although the Emperor Septimius Severus is believed to have ended their participation around 200 AD, in the 1st and 2nd centuries women were permitted to become gladiators, and many joined men in fighting and hunting in the Colosseum.

- 44 -

How quickly can you solve this crossword?

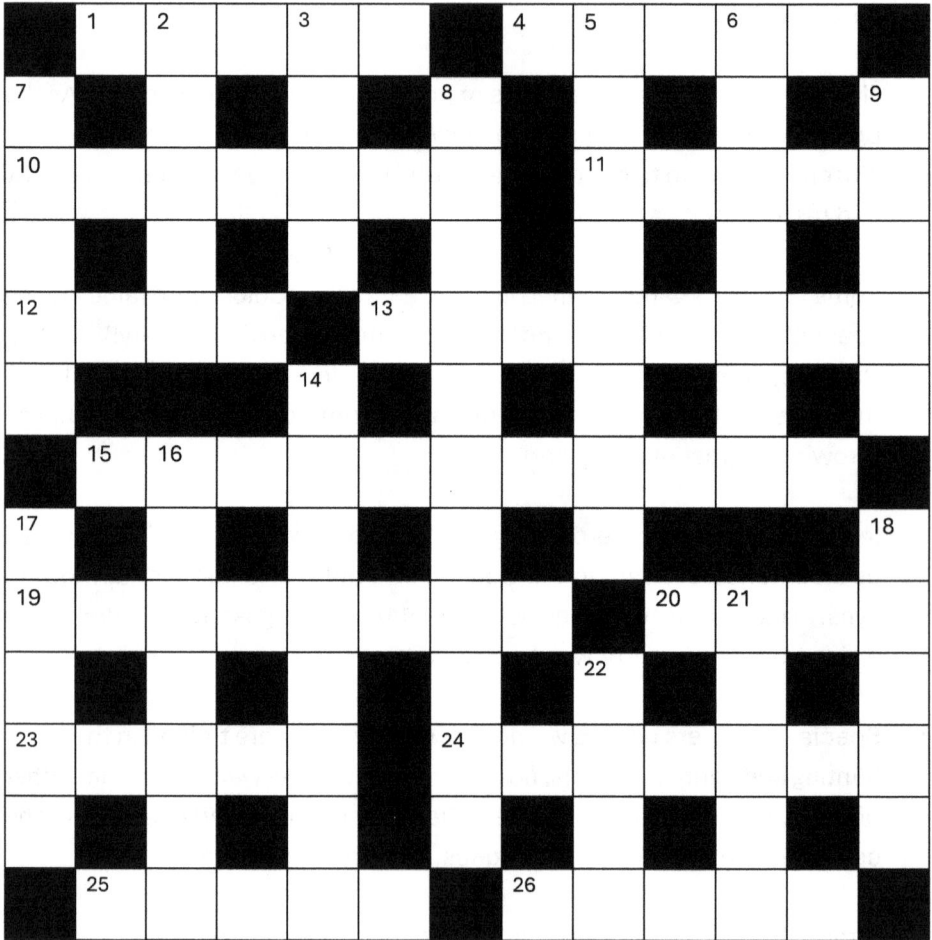

ACROSS

1. Less perilous
4. Heroism
10. Largest elephant species
11. Airman
12. Exchanges money for
13. Keep going
15. Terminus, end of a trip
19. Teaches
20. Cab
23. Open a knot
24. Making money
25. Medical images
26. Haste, rapidity

DOWN

2. Range
3. Per
5. Desire for food
6. Florida city
7. Gleeful
8. Met
9. Stallion, charger
14. Tactic
16. 0° line of latitude
17. Location of an event
18. Vocalizes musically
21. Similar
22. Let slip from the hands

The eight single-digit numbers below have been removed from this magic square.

Place the numbers back in the grid so that the four boxes in each row and in each column total 40.

2 3 4 5 6 7 8 9

	12	17	
16			13
	19	10	
11			18

THE ACTOR WHO WAS NOMINATED FOR TWO OSCARS FOR THE SAME ROLE

The Academy Awards are very much the highlight of each year's movie awards season. Since the late 1920s, cinema fans the world over have turned their eyes to Hollywood at the beginning of the year to find out who will take away one of the most coveted prizes in any creative industry.

Over the decades, of course, the Oscars have seen their fair share of shocks, firsts, records, and superlatives. The longest Best Picture winner, for instance, is still 1939's *Gone With The Wind*, which clocks in at just under 4 hours. When he won the Best Actor Oscar for his role in *The Father*, 83-year-old Sir Anthony Hopkins became the oldest performer to win a competitive Oscar in the awards' history. At the other end of the scale, Tatum O'Neal was just 10 when she won the Best Supporting Actress award for *Paper Moon* in 1973. And when Peter Finch won the Best Actor Oscar for his role in *Network* in 1977, he had the unfortunate honor of being the first person to win an acting Oscar after their death; sadly, he had passed away just two months before the ceremony, at the age of only 60. One of the strangest quirks the Oscars have ever seen, however, took place way back in 1945.

Born in Dublin in 1888, Irish actor Barry Fitzgerald initially worked as a banker before being drawn into the theatre in Ireland and eventually making his way to Hollywood in the 1920s. His career slowly flourished, and over the next three decades Fitzgerald established himself as one of the greatest character actors of his day. In 1944, his movie career culminated in a starring role opposite the Hollywood legend Bing Crosby in his latest comedy musical, *Going My Way*.

The film told the story of a grizzled and traditional New York priest, played by Fitzgerald, whose quiet world is turned upside down by the arrival of a younger, brasher, more carefree priest, played by Crosby. *Going My Way* was a great success, and as well as being widely considered one of Bing Crosby's finest movies, it went into the 1945 Oscars with 10 nominations—including two for Fitzgerald.

Oddly, for his role in *Going My Way*, Fitzgerald found himself nominated both as the film's lead actor (alongside Bing Crosby, who was also nominated as Best Actor), and as its Best Supporting Actor. That understandably made him the first person in the Academy Awards' history to receive separate nominations for exactly the same performance—and theoretically, made it possible for him to take home both the Best Actor and Best Supporting Actor statuettes on the same night, for the same role.

As it happens, *Going My Way* won in seven of its 10 nominated categories—with Bing Crosby taking the lead actor's award, and Fitzgerald winning the supporting award alongside him. But the entire debacle of Fitzgerald's multiple nominations had shown that there was a bizarre loophole in the Oscar's nominating and voting schedule that, until then, did indeed allow the same person to be nominated in more than one category for the same performance. That loophole was thankfully closed and has remained closed ever since, giving Fitzgerald not only his Oscar, but a truly unique place in Oscar history.

TOP 6 · FACTS
THE OSCARS

- The very first Academy Awards were held in May 1929. There were originally just 12 awards categories (including separate awards for comedy and dramatic directing), and winners were told of their victory three months before the ceremony; the event was therefore just a chance for winners to turn up and receive their awards.

- At the first Oscars, Warner Brothers Studios were awarded a special award for producing the first commercial sound film, or "talkie," *The Jazz Singer*. The first winner of Best Picture, however, was a silent movie, *Wings*.

- The 19th Academy Awards in 1946 was the first time members of the public were allowed to purchase tickets to the event and sit in the audience.

- Walt Disney remains the most successful person at the Oscars, winning a total of 22 competitive awards, plus an additional four special or honorary awards for his achievements in animation and cinema. In total, he received a staggering 59 nominations throughout his career.

- The first Black performer to win an Oscar was Hattie McDaniel, who won the Best Supporting Actress award for her role in 1939's epic *Gone with the Wind*. With segregation still in force in the United States at the time, however, McDaniel had to sit at the very back of the theatre and was not permitted to sit with the rest of her castmates on the night of her win.

- Although some actors and actresses like to enjoy their time in the spotlight (despite music now being played to usher them off stage after 45 seconds!), some Oscar winners have kept their speeches brief. One of the shortest was the great director Alfred Hitchcock, who despite one of the most illustrious directing careers in Hollywood history never won a competitive award. The Academy finally redressed the oversight in 1968 and bestowed on Hitchcock their special Irving G. Thalberg Memorial Award—an honorary award recognizing a lifetime of cinematic achievement. Hitchcock approached the microphone with his award in hand, and simply said, "Thank you."

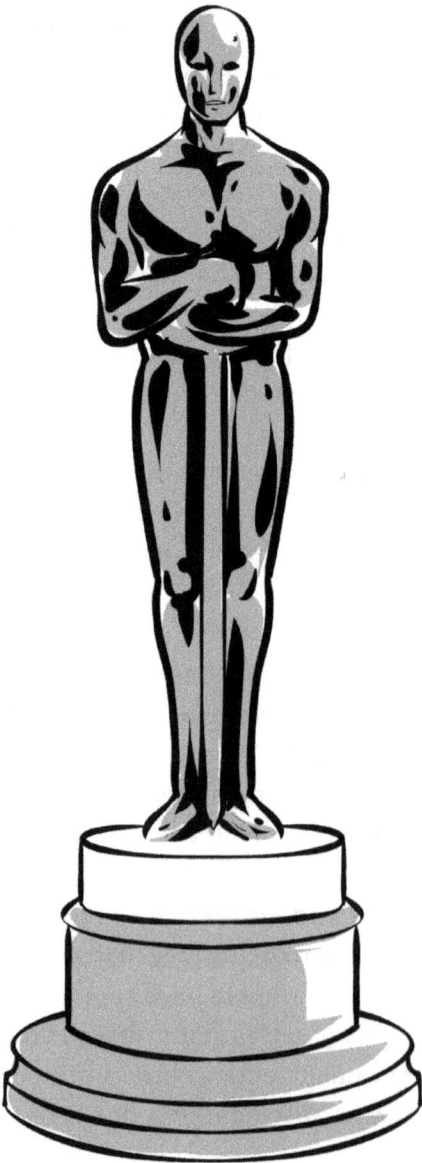

46

Fill in the grid below so that each row of nine squares, each column of nine squares, and each smaller 3 x 3 set of nine squares contain the digits 1–9 once and only once.

There can be no duplicate digits in any row, column, or smaller square.

Can you complete the grid correctly?

						9		3
		1	6	4		8	5	7
				3				
	7	9	5		4	3		
2				9	7			
	4	5			3			9
8		6		1	9		3	
9	1		3		6			
7		3	4		8			

Can you find your way through this maze from top to bottom?

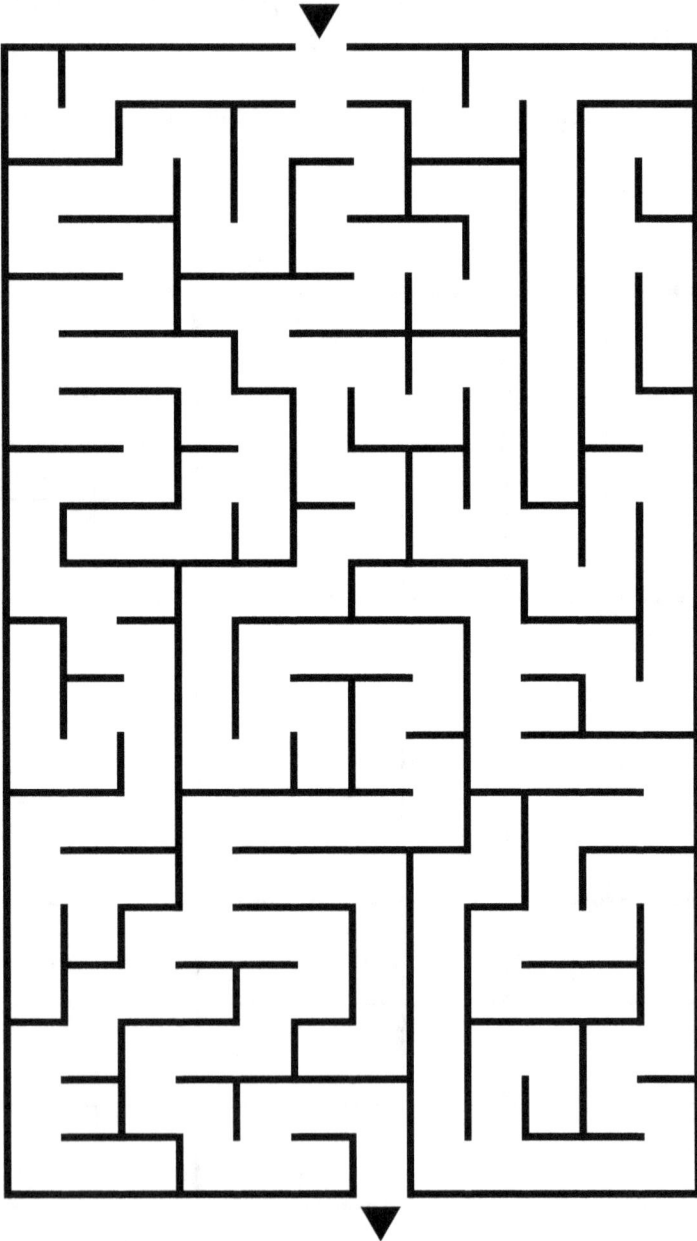

HOW CHARLES DICKENS ENDED UP IN JAIL

I f you've ever read a Charles Dickens novel or seen one of his many stories adapted for the big screen, you'll know that one of the themes of his work is the intense poverty and social injustice that he saw all around him in British Victorian society. As well as concocting remarkably intricate soap opera-style plots—featuring multiple intertwined characters, hilarious comic caricatures, and moments of shocking high drama—Dickens was as much a social commentator as an author and used the fame his books gave him to educate his well-to-do friends and fans on what life was truly like for the very poorest people at the time. But Dickens did not have to imagine what life was like for those on the bottom rung of society, as he had witnessed it first-hand. In fact, long before he made it as an author and became perhaps the most famous and successful writer of the day, as a child he had endured a brief but horrific spell in prison alongside the rest of his poverty-stricken family.

One of eight children born to his parents John and Elizabeth, Charles Dickens was born in the city of Portsmouth, on England's south coast, in 1812. The young family relocated to London in 1822, where John took a job as a naval pay clerk—a fairly well-paid and well-respected position at the time that would likely have provided enough for the family to live off; by the standards of the day, in fact, they would have easily been considered middle class. Unfortunately, despite his job, John was terrible with money and would frequently overspend and fall behind on debts and repayments. As a result, in 1824 he was sent to Marshalsea, an infamous debtors' prison on the south bank of London's river Thames, for failing to repay a debt to a local baker of forty pounds and ten shillings—and as was often the case at the time, his entire family was forced to join him.

Dickens and his siblings were ultimately (and rather embarrassingly) withdrawn from school and unceremoniously taken to Marshalsea alongside their father and mother. Conditions in the prison were grim, as there was no national prison service in England at the time and institutions like that were typically run by private corporations looking to profit off the poorest and least fortunate.

Prisoners who could afford to pay or bribe their guards would be rewarded with separate quarters, lighter chains and shackles, better food, and all manner of other "easements." Dickens' family, however, was at the poorer end of the scale, and as a result Charles was taken from his family and forced to work in a factory that made boot-blacking polish at the age of just 12.

Eventually, the family was released from prison (and Marshalsea went on to close during Dickens' lifetime, in 1842). His experiences there, however, stayed with Dickens forever. In his novel *Little Dorrit*, the title character, Amy, is born and raised at Marshalsea, before the family is rescued from poverty by a sudden twist of circumstances; her description of life in the prison is very much based on Dickens' own life. As his career blossomed and Dickens went on to become a very wealthy man in Victorian high-society, he continued to use his work to shine a light on what he saw and experienced in Marshalsea and beyond, with his books continuing to give us an idea of what life was like back then even today.

TOP 6 · FACTS
CHARLES DICKENS

- Charles Dickens did not originally want to be an author, but an actor. After his books became successful, however, he would often indulge his love of theatre by giving live readings of his stories in which he would play every character, putting on all the different voices and accents required.

- Dickens wrote his first novel when he was just 24 years old. *The Pickwick Papers* was an almost instant success; divided into a series of chapters published in a magazine one after the other, the circulation of his story rose from 400 copies a month to over 40,000 by the end of the story!

- In 1847, Dickens commissioned a family friend to paint a portrait of his wife, Catherine. The following year, it was put on display at London's prestigious Royal Academy, but the title of the picture—"Mrs. Charles Dickens"—was misspelled, and the picture was displayed under Dickens' name, "Mr. Charles Dickens." According to legend, many of the visitors who came to see the picture believed it to be a picture of Dickens in drag!

- Dickens was an animal lover and kept a pet raven called Grip. He wrote the bird into one of his novels, *Barnaby Rudge*.

- In 1865, Dickens was traveling home to London from France, when his train derailed while crossing a bridge, sending several carriages tumbling down into the river below. Fortunately, Dickens was unharmed, and despite being 53 years old at the time, bravely helped to rescue passengers from the waters—before climbing back onto the bridge to retrieve the final chapter of his book, *Our Mutual Friend*, from his compartment!

- After his death, Dickens had requested a quiet funeral, with no public announcement, and to be buried simply in the churchyard of Rochester Cathedral in Kent. Proving how popular and loved a figure he had become, however, after his death in 1870 Dickens was buried in a special writers' area of Westminster Abbey in London, known as Poet's Corner, while a full procession through the city was arranged so that hundreds of thousands of fans could come to pay their respects.

- 48 -

Dim the lights and light some candles... It's time for a nice, relaxing soak in the tub!

BATH BOMB
CLOSE YOUR EYES
FOAM
LOOFAH
SOAP

BATH SALTS
DIMMED LIGHTS
GOOD BOOK
RELAXING MUSIC
SOOTHING

BUBBLES
ESSENTIAL OILS
HOT WATER
SCENTED CANDLE
WASHCLOTH

```
X  P  B  M  O  B  H  T  A  B  N  N  P  Z  G  T  V
S  O  I  A  R  A  X  D  K  F  C  G  G  O  X  M  D
U  E  S  E  Y  E  R  U  O  Y  E  S  O  L  C  S  J
B  N  L  R  E  T  A  W  T  O  H  D  D  S  L  H  A
K  Y  G  B  Y  I  V  S  R  Q  B  R  C  I  C  E  M
U  H  M  I  B  J  G  L  T  O  W  E  O  I  E  F  L
T  X  X  A  V  U  X  G  O  L  N  L  S  B  C  T  R
D  T  F  C  Q  A  B  K  N  T  A  U  Y  E  Z  F  I
M  O  V  P  X  V  I  U  E  I  M  S  P  A  O  S  S
E  Z  L  C  A  M  H  D  T  G  H  L  H  S  F  B  D
B  P  O  E  A  Q  C  N  N  M  O  T  N  T  J  B  I
N  D  Q  O  F  A  E  I  W  O  C  R  O  B  A  C  I
G  H  F  W  N  S  X  H  F  V  V  B  T  O  P  B  Y
X  S  A  D  S  A  V  A  K  Z  K  H  A  N  S  V  Y
B  U  L  E  L  Z  H  P  Q  Y  K  A  Z  Z  W  Y  C
R  E  B  E  S  T  H  G  I  L  D  E  M  M  I  D  E
I  S  R  F  K  B  V  R  W  A  S  H  C  L  O  T  H
```

What two-word phrase can be read from the figure below?

THINK

Each of the letters in the quotation below has been swapped for another. Can you decode the message?

"IAXI'Z IAM MZZMCDM BP RF
XDISCN:
"__ A _'_ __E __S____ __ M_
____N_:

S'R SCIMVMZIMJ SC EAXI SI EBKYJ
UM
_'_ __T_R_____ __ __A_ __
W__L_ __

YSTM IB UM FBK." – RMVFY ZIVMMG
_I__ __ B_ _O_." – ___Y_
____E_

THE LAST SURVIVOR OF THE CRIMEAN WAR WAS A TORTOISE

The Crimean War was a brutal conflict that erupted mainly around the Crimean Peninsula on the Black Sea in 1853. It was fought by an alliance of European powers—the United Kingdom, France, Sardinia, and the Ottoman Empire, a vast empire in the southeast corner of Europe including much of modern-day Turkey and Greece—against Russia, who saw the fall of the Ottoman Empire as an opportunity to advance its powers across the Black Sea region. The western European nations, however, saw an increasingly powerful Russia as a threat and so entered the war as a means of ensuring a power balance across the continent. For the next two and a half years this western and Ottoman alliance fought back hard against the advancing Russian powers, eventually securing victory in the spring of 1856.

The toll of the war was considerable, even by 19th century standards. More than one million men were sent to the war, of which a staggering 600,000 lost their lives; Russia alone lost as many as 450,000 of its troops. But conditions were so bad that relatively few of those lives were lost on the battlefield; instead, many soldiers succumbed to disease, or else a lack of appropriate medical treatment. In fact, it has been estimated that of the 160,000 British, French, Italian and Ottoman lives lost, two out of every three died away from the frontline of the war.

Alongside the lives lost, however, there were many extraordinary stories of survivors. And perhaps the most curious of all those happened to be that of the longest-lived survivor of the entire war, who did not die until 2004, at the age of 160. If that sounds too bizarre to be true, though, realize this: the longest-lived survivor of Crimea was a gigantic tortoise!

Timothy the tortoise is believed to have been born somewhere around the Ottoman peninsula in the 1840s. A Portuguese vessel adopted him as its mascot, and in 1854 he was found on board a private ship in Mediterranean waters and adopted by a British royal navy captain, John Guy Courtenay-Everard. Over the next few decades, Timothy continued to act as a ship's mascot, sailing into the bombardment of Sevastopol, at the height of the Crimean War, on board the British gunship HMS *Queen*.

After his life in the military, however, towards the end of the 1800s Timothy was taken back to the UK and lived in the gardens of Powderham Castle, near Exeter, in rural southwest England. In 1924—now well into his 80s!—an effort was made to mate Timothy to provide a new generation of tortoises at the castle. It was at this point that it was discovered that "Timothy" was actually a female!

By now something of a celebrity at the castle, for the next eight decades Timothy continued to live at Powderham, before his (or rather, her) death in 2004. Although estimates of her age could never be fully accurate, she was thought to have been around 160 years old at the time, making her not only the oldest resident of Great Britain but the longest-lived survivor of one of Europe's most significant and brutal wars.

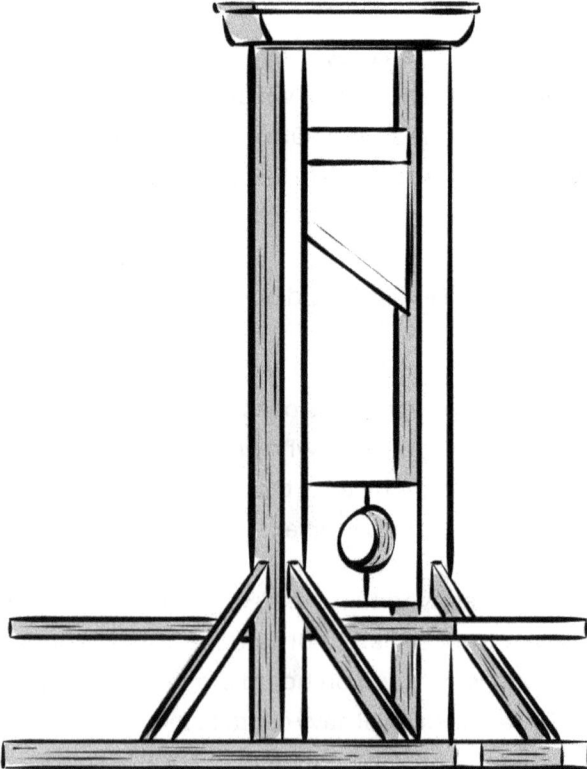

TOP 6 · FACTS
FAMOUS LASTS

- Once one of the biggest video rental brands in the world, the last Blockbuster video store remains open and operational in the town of Bend, Oregon. It has since become something of a tourist attraction, and visitors can purchase t-shirts (as well as rent movies) at the store, bearing the words "The Last Blockbuster"!

- At the height of its popularity in the 1920s, the Western Union telegram service was delivering a staggering 200 million messages every day. As telephones (and then online communication) gradually ate away at the service's use, however, the telegram network dwindled; the very last one was sent on January 27, 2006.

- Towards the end of the Second World War, at around 8 o'clock in the morning on May 7, 1945, a US tank battalion was ambushed by a German Panzer unit in northern Czechoslovakia. One of the men, Private 1st Class Charles Havlat, from Nebraska, was shot in the head and killed; just a matter of minutes earlier, the German forces had officially surrendered to the Allies and the war had officially ended. The message had yet to be communicated across Europe, however, and as a result Havlat became the final casualty of the war.

- When the comedy series M*A*S*H came to an end in 1983, some 120 million Americans tuned in to watch the final 2½ hour episode, "Goodbye, Farewell and Amen"—the largest audience to date for a single episode of television.

- The last person executed in France using the guillotine was a Tunisian man named Hamida Djandoubi—in 1977!

- Everyone knows that Neil Armstrong was the first man to set foot on the Moon back in 1969. To date, however, the last man to walk on the Moon was US astronaut Eugene Cernan, known as Gene, who was part of the Apollo 17 mission in 1972.

- 50 -
BATHROOM GAME: WORD TILES

The names of 11 feature-length Disney animated movies, past and present, are hidden in the grid below—but not in straight lines! Can you find all the names so that no letter is used more than once, and no letter is left over? The first has been filled in for you to make a start.

B	A	P	O	C	A	S	N	O	W
R	M	B	B	E	H	S	E	T	W
O	D	I	U	A	O	L	A	I	H
B	O	D	T	Y	N	E	L	D	I
I	O	U	N	A	T	E	A	D	N
N	H	M	D	T	A	P	U	T	Y
T	O	B	E	H	S	I	A	E	B
S	A	E	B	H	E	N	G	B	O
I	N	C	H	T	L	N	K	T	L
P	O	C	I	O	I	O	I	N	G

The 16 words and phrases in the grid below can be arranged into four connected groups of four—that is, with each set of four answers having something in common.

Can you work out the connections? Be careful, though—some answers might belong in more than one group, but there is only one overall solution!

Sigh	Gasp	Buckle	Latch
Wasp	Unclasp	Demolish	Exhale
Key	Inhale	Grasp	Bolt
Rasp	Devour	Clasp	Breathe

CONCLUSION

And so, with that final fiendish connecting puzzle, your *Ultimate Crapper Companion* is complete!

Over the past 100 pages here, we've journeyed through 5,000 years of history, taken a voyage to the depths of the jungle and the bottom of the sea, joined a gladiatorial duo on the floor of the Colosseum, and went to prison with one of the world's most famous and celebrated authors.

We've learned about the White House's whiteness and the bizarre animals that once called it home. We've found out about the ancient tortoise that once sailed into battle (before dying in an English country garden more than a century and a half later!) And we've found out what you can do with an uncoiled spring, a weak adhesive, and a little bit of coal tar and a dirty petri dish. We've even discovered how not to kill a flock of emus!

Along the way here, of course, we've tested your puzzle-solving skills, your logical and lateral thinking skills, and more than a little of your general knowledge, too—all while you were likely doing little more than sitting on the toilet!

All in all, it's hoped that this book has been anything but a waste of time; in fact, it's hopefully allowed you to turn what might otherwise have *been* wasted time into something far more entertaining, more informative, and most important of all, more fun!

SOLUTIONS

- 1 -

R	E	Q	U	E	S	T	■	A	U	R	A	S
A	■	U	■	V	■	A	■	G	■	O	■	C
I	C	E	R	I	N	K	■	A	L	T	A	R
L	■	E	■	D	■	I	■	I	■	A	■	I
S	E	N	S	E	■	N	O	N	S	T	O	P
■	■	■	■	N	■	G	■	■	■	E	■	T
S	P	R	I	T	E	■	M	I	S	S	E	S
U	■	E	■	■	■	S	■	N	■	■	■	■
B	U	F	F	A	L	O	■	S	I	L	L	Y
J	■	U	■	T	■	R	■	T	■	I	■	A
E	A	S	E	L	■	T	R	A	F	F	I	C
C	■	E	■	A	■	O	■	L	■	T	■	H
T	A	S	K	S	■	F	I	L	M	S	E	T

- 3 -

4	5	1	6	7	8	3	9	2
7	8	3	2	9	1	4	6	5
6	2	9	5	3	4	8	1	7
5	4	8	1	6	7	2	3	9
9	3	2	4	8	5	1	7	6
1	6	7	3	2	9	5	8	4
3	9	6	8	5	2	7	4	1
2	7	4	9	1	3	6	5	8
8	1	5	7	4	6	9	2	3

- 2 -

▼

W	H	I	L	E
N	A	M	E	S
S	T	A	T	E
U	R	G	E	D
P	R	I	N	T
M	O	N	T	H
T	H	E	I	R

Man in the Moon

- 4 -

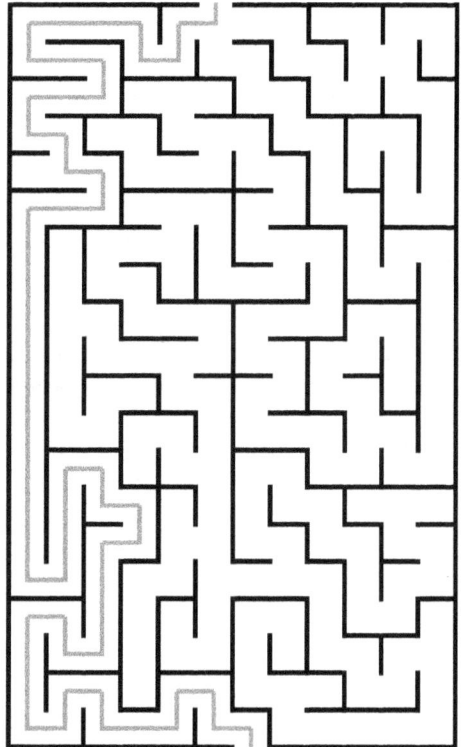

- 5 -

```
U V E J S T O I L E T N C J K T J
S B C M R P Y X T G R K T X Q W K
T R A P I W M E W E S T H B U J X
R B Y T E R C K W M C E D Z M S L
E O Q S H U R O U Z F D B H E Z Z
S K E Q A T H O A M R I A H B Y D
N Q M F A S U J R D C B X B M I C
E C U K Z K B B J P X N D C U A S
P W Y H K O L L Z R K N I S B A I
S G Z F I N I X T W O S M I F V T
I P S L M K A W L M T T N G G W S
D X E T P A R T N E J E A U E G N
P R O N J X L D R K T D B I X V T
A A A L G O E N N E P P N R D R F
O B W U J V W I X H T R T E D A V
S W M M K O O K M B B A S I N L R
T D I F S Q T S G D N Q W P C L K
```

- 7 -

```
                        B O B
                        L
              B E N U M B       B
                        R   A   E
      B       B A T H T U B   C D
      R       A           K   A A
      O       T       B   B O O K C L U B
      K       H       R         O   B
      E       B       E     B O M B
      N   B A O B A B D           B
      R           M   C
  B I C A R B     M   R
      B           C
              B U L B
              M
              B A N D B
```

- 6 -

FOLKLORE

- 8 -

There are 16 squares in total

Three-dimensional

- 9 -

```
R E C E I P T I
R O L L I V E M
T D O M A C R E
S N T R I H E S
A A S G N I D C
E R D N E N I E
H A E P P A S N
T R O N I R U T
```

- 10 -

Clockwise

- 11 -

Rafael Nadal – Tennis
Travis Kelce – American football
Sebastian Vettel – Motor racing
Simone Biles – Gymnastics
Michael Phelps – Swimming
Nikola Jokic – Basketball
Aaron Judge – Baseball
Lionel Messi – Soccer

- 12 -

"Who I am on stage is very, very different to who I am in real life."
– Beyonce

Sail the seven seas

- 13 -

1. Albany, Santa Fe
2. Folklore, Lover
3. Jupiter, Venus
4. Banana, Lemon
5. Hood, Umbrella
6. Blanket, Quilt

- 14 -

9	12	16	2
15	3	8	13
4	18	10	7
11	6	5	17

- 15 -

	S	M	O	K	E		A	S	K	E	D	
P	O		I		T		A		M		M	
R	E	V	E	N	G	E		T	E	E	N	Y
I		I		G		M		U		R		T
D	E	E	P		A	P	P	R	O	A	C	H
E				T		E		D		L		S
	N	E	T	H	E	R	L	A	N	D	S	
U		A		I		A		Y				S
S	T	R	E	N	G	T	H		A	L	S	O
U		L		K		U		E		O		R
A	L	I	B	I		R	E	C	O	V	E	R
L		E		N		E		H		E		Y
	B	R	A	G	S		L	O	O	S	E	

- 16 -

CORVIDS:

Jackdaw, Magpie, Jay, Raven

WORDS WITH SILENT FIRST LETTERS:

Knight, Wrath, Pterodactyl, Gnome

GARDEN FEATURES AND FIXTURES:

Lawn, Flamingo, Sundial, Pond

CHESS PIECES:

Queen, Bishop, Rook, Pawn

- 17 -

4	5	6	2	9	3	7	8	1
7	8	1	4	6	5	3	9	2
3	2	9	8	1	7	5	4	6
6	1	5	7	4	2	8	3	9
8	9	3	6	5	1	2	7	4
2	7	4	9	3	8	6	1	5
9	6	7	5	8	4	1	2	3
1	4	2	3	7	6	9	5	8
5	3	8	1	2	9	4	6	7

- 18 -

Left-hand drive

T	I	L	E	D
H	■	L	■	I
R	E	A	C	T
O	■	M	■	T
B	R	A	V	O

- 19 -

- 20 -

1. J (First letter of months in order, starting with February)
2. U (Staring at A, missing one, two, three, four, then five letters out of the alphabet)
3. X (Last letters of one, two, three, four, five, and six)

▼

F	R	O	T	H
S	T	U	F	F
W	A	T	E	R
F	U	S	S	Y
C	L	I	M	B
T	O	D	A	Y
C	H	E	C	K

- 22 -

L I C E N S E D T O K I L L
L O . . . . O
Y . L U L L . . . . G
A . O . O I
L . L . S C
. . L . T . L . . . . . A
L O V E R S Q U A R R E L
. W . . . O . N L
. C . . . U . D I
. A . . L A W F U L . . . B
. L . . . . . I . . . . . E
. . L . . . . L E G P U L L
L I V E R P O O L
. . N
L A T I T U D I N A L
. . I
. . L

- 23 -

1. Elbow
2. Brain
3. Heart
4. Stomach
5. Hand
6. Pancreas
7. Muscle
8. Tendon

J	U	M	P	A	R	I	S
O	C	A	L	O	T	T	P
L	R	A	N	D	I	E	A
U	G	T	I	S	R	R	R
F	N	O	R	E	A	Y	E
H	I	R	E	T	S	E	A
T	L	I	O	T	S	A	T
U	O	Y	T	S	A	N	E

- 25 -

"I've been working since I was nine. I've never known a life without a film set!"
– Daniel Radcliffe

Time and time again

- 26 -

Venice – Italy
Shanghai – China
Edinburgh – Scotland
Istanbul – Turkey
Guadalajara – Mexico
Rio de Janeiro – Brazil
Nice – France
Vancouver – Canada

27

▼

N	O	V	E	L
T	H	I	N	K
S	I	N	C	E
S	T	E	P	S
V	E	G	A	N
S	H	A	L	L
F	O	R	C	E

An eye for an eye, a tooth for a tooth

- 28 -

1. Bishop, Queen
2. Organ, Piano
3. Basil, Oregano
4. Airplane, Bird
5. Eleven, Five
6. Cuba, Jamaica

- 29 -

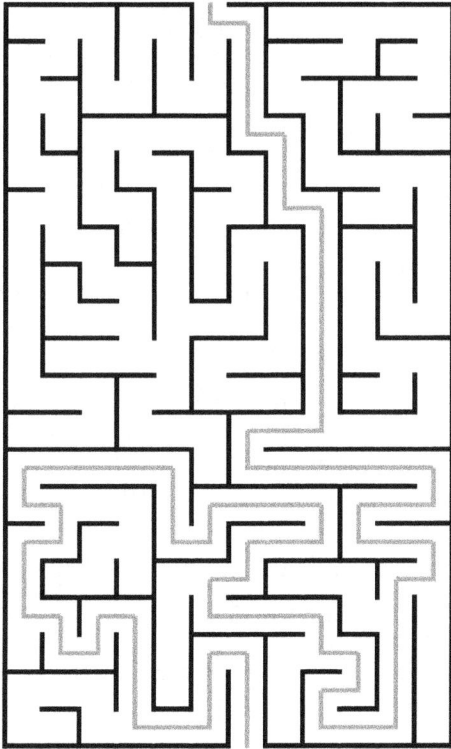

Truman, Biden, Adams, Washington, Jefferson, Buchanan, Monroe, Hayes, Obama, McKinley, Roosevelt, Van Buren, Cleveland, Jackson.

- 31 -

10	13	16	3
15	4	9	14
5	18	11	8
12	7	6	17

- 32 -

5	4	8	6	7	2	9	3	1
2	7	3	8	1	9	5	6	4
9	6	1	4	5	3	7	2	8
4	1	2	7	6	5	3	8	9
6	8	9	1	3	4	2	5	7
3	5	7	2	9	8	4	1	6
7	2	4	3	8	6	1	9	5
8	3	5	9	4	1	6	7	2
1	9	6	5	2	7	8	4	3

- 30 -

T	R	U	M	I	D	E	N	A	D
W	A	S	A	B	N	R	B	U	A
N	O	H	N	M	O	O	E	C	M
H	T	I	J	E	F	O	B	H	S
A	G	N	R	E	F	M	A	A	N
Y	E	S	S	O	N	C	M	A	A
R	O	O	N	V	A	K	L	E	N
V	E	S	O	B	N	I	C	V	D
E	L	T	S	U	R	N	Y	E	N
J	A	C	K	N	E	L	E	L	A

159

- 33 -

M	A	Y	B	E	■	S	■	P
E	■	A	A	C	T	I	O	N
D	E	C	O	R	■	A	■	I
I	■	H	T	I	T	A	N	S
A	C	T	■	H	E	■	T	
■	O	S	C	■	A	S	K	
D	Y	N	A	M	O	■	R	■ E
■	O	T	■	A	N	I	M	E
E	T	H	I	C	S	■	S	■ P
■	E	N	T	E	E	N	S	

35

C	E	L	L	P	H	O	N	E
C	O	U	R	T	S	H	I	P
O	R	C	H	E	S	T	R	A
E	D	I	T	O	R	I	A	L
C	H	I	L	D	C	A	R	E
P	L	A	I	N	T	I	F	F

- 34 -

```
N Z C U R L I N G I R O N W F I K
D O O P M A H S D O Z V A Q M N H
F H A I R S P R A Y R X P W B Q X
T O C E X Y C R O F E E J I M W Z
S X R O P Z R R P Y Y U I B L A I
T B T I N F X C W T R S K P Q Y R
R C Z R D D C M E V D Y A U P O P
A H H F W X I M B Z R I B E M A E
I S C A L P Z T D C I L N J D S R
G M J C D U X E R A H E U F C M
H C R B A R A B S O H L Y Q A L B
T H Z K M H E I R D N E X B M O C
E J J Q A C J L S H K E W J D V J
N K O A W L E G R T M R R V G F E
E E L C I L L O F U Y W B K E S O
R F X O E S H D U E C L O J M S I
S R X D B L O W D R Y N E B E P W
```

- 36 -

- 37 -

THINGS THAT HAVE KEYS:
Lock, Piano, Car, Door
CREATURES IN DISNEY ANIMATION TITLE:
Hound, Mermaid, Lion, Beast
BLACK AND WHITE THINGS:
Old movie, Panda, Zebra, Dalmatian
MYTHICAL CREATURES:
Unicorn, Cyclops, Fairy, Phoenix

B	R	U	I	S	E	A	G
L	Y	E	S	A	U	C	L
R	I	E	S	T	W	E	E
A	N	M	B	E	O	R	S
E	I	U	S	R	U	E	E
S	T	N	U	R	T	S	V
O	N	A	R	U	A	T	E
O	N	R	A	E	C	I	N

- 41 -

A						
		D			D	E
		B	A		C	
C					E	B

- 39 -

"'Magic' is who I am on the basketball court. Earvin is who I am."
– Magic Johnson

Free for all

- 42 -

1. Arial, Comic Sans
2. Qatar, Syria
3. Chiefs, Eagles
4. Lettuce, Tomato
5. Doormat, Rug
6. Chameleon, Iguana

- 40 -

Earl Grey – Tea
Ciabatta – Bread
Pinto – Bean
Pistachio – Nut
Cappuccino – Coffee
Golden Delicious – Apple
Beaujolais – Wine
Minestrone – Soup

- 43 -

1. Piano
2. Trumpet
3. Triangle
4. Flute
5. Cello
6. Mandolin
7. Tuba
8. Organ

- 44 -

	S	A	F	E	R		V	A	L	O	R	
H		R		A		E		P		R		S
A	F	R	I	C	A	N		P	I	L	O	T
P		A		H		C		E		A		E
P	A	Y	S		C	O	N	T	I	N	U	E
Y			S		U		I		D			D
	D	E	S	T	I	N	A	T	I	O	N	
V		Q		R		T		E				S
E	D	U	C	A	T	E	S		T	A	X	I
N		A		T		R		D		L		N
U	N	T	I	E		E	A	R	N	I	N	G
E		O		G		D		O		K		S
	X	R	A	Y	S		S	P	E	E	D	

- 46 -

4	6	2	7	8	5	9	1	3
3	9	1	6	4	2	8	5	7
5	8	7	9	3	1	2	4	6
1	7	9	5	6	4	3	2	8
2	3	8	1	9	7	4	6	5
6	4	5	8	2	3	1	7	9
8	5	6	2	1	9	7	3	4
9	1	4	3	7	6	5	8	2
7	2	3	4	5	8	6	9	1

- 45 -

9	12	17	2
16	3	8	13
4	19	10	7
11	6	5	18

- 47 -

162

- 48 -

- 49 -

Think outside of the box

"That's the essence of my acting: I'm interested in what it would be like to be you." – Meryl Streep

- 50 -

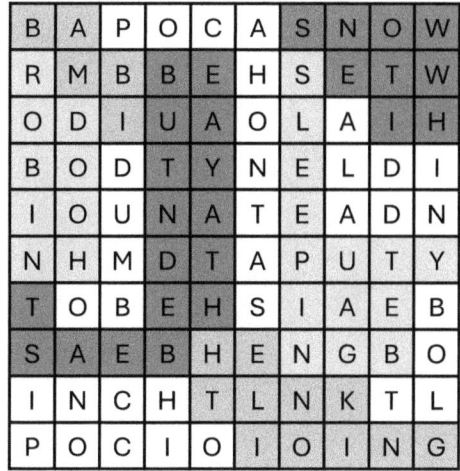

Bambi, Pocahontas, Snow White, Robin Hood, Beauty and the Beast, Sleeping Beauty, Dumbo, Aladdin, The Lion King, Bolt, Pinocchio

- 51 -

MOVEMENTS OF THE LUNGS:
Sigh, Gasp, Exhale, Breathe
FASTENERS:
Buckle, Latch, Key, Clasp
WORDS ENDING –ASP:
Wasp, Unclasp, Grasp, Rasp
EATING QUICKLY AND GREEDILY:
Demolish, Inhale, Bolt, Devour

www.ingramcontent.com/pod-product-compliance
Lightning Source LLC
Chambersburg PA
CBHW051733020426
42333CB00014B/1284